PROCRASTINATION

The Opportunity Killer

Author

Dr. Amit Abraham

F-2/16, Ansari Road, Daryaganj, New Delhi-110002
☎ 011-23275434, 23262683, 23250704 • *Fax:* 011-23257790
E-mail: info@unicornbooks.in • *Website:* www.unicornbooks.in

Branch : Mumbai

23-25, Zaoba Wadi, Thakurdwar, Mumbai-401002

☎ 022-22010941, 022-22053387

E-mail: rapidex@bom5.vsnl.net.in

Showroom :

★ **PM Publications,** New Delhi

- 10-B, Netaji Subhash Marg, Daryaganj
  New Delhi-110002
- 6686, Khari Baoli, Delhi-110006

ISBN 978-81-7806-337-9

Procrastination The Opportunity Killer

Edition: July 2013

Printed at : Param Offsetters, Okhla, New Delhi-110020

Acknowledgements

I will not procrastinate in saying thanks to all those who directly and indirectly helped and motivated me to finish a work which I had begun ages back. Some hindrance or the other kept cropping up and I kept procrastinating, first beginning with writing this book and then at various stages completing its chapters. However, finally I overcame this procrastinating behaviour of mine and got down to finishing the work I had begun with great zeal.

I thank most of my friends on facebook for helping me collect data through online surveys. These surveys gave me insight into many things which I had not even thought of about procrastinating behaviour. Who says interacting through social networking sites only leads one to procrastinate other works – they can be used for constructive purposes as well along with cyber socializing.

I thank my students who undertook different research studies in collaboration with me to study the cause and effect relationship of procrastination with various variables. The data collected and the statistical analysis of the same helped me a lot in writing this book and developing a scale to measure procrastination.

I would like to thank someone very special who despite my repeated requests kept procrastinating responding to surveys I had posted but kept asking me daily about the status of my writing work. Many times people help you in manners which are really unique.

With all this procrastination I have done and been busy writing about my family kept procrastinating its various activities from time to time. I really need to thank my wife and daughter for bearing with me these procrastinations.

Finally, a word of thanks to the publishers. They were the only ones who did not procrastinate in accepting this book for publication.

Dr. Amit Abraham
samvaidna@hotmail.com

Preface

There are various social, personality and psychological causes of procrastination, all of which can be individually identified, assessed, treated and overcome through the development of a high action identity, a positive mentality, a genuine desire to pursue goals, effective self-regulation and through active self-affirmation that increases self-efficacy. It is crucial for one's physical and psychological health to treat and overcome this irrational self-sabotaging behaviour. While there are numerous causes of and treatments for procrastination, the most important step to overcoming procrastination is to become self aware of any procrastinator tendencies.

The primary manifestations of self-handicapping through procrastination include excessive sleeping, watching television, playing computer games, social activities and disruptions, alcohol and other drug use, environmental handicaps, music, noise distraction and having a cluttered and disorganized living space. However, procrastination is not simply an illustration of laziness, indifference or poor time management, but a complex self-defeating behaviour attributed to several primary causes. Procrastination must be understood within the context of various interrelated emotions, cognitions, behaviour', personality traits and psychological and social determinants. Be on the watch out if you exhibit any of these manifestations – you need to be reading this book.

This book is so written that you not only become educated about procrastination but also able to measure yourself on the various psychological variables which lead to procrastinating behaviour. This book helps you identify those variables and suggests remedial measures to practise and adopt. In fact, this book is about the psychology of procrastination and the procrastinator. So, take full advantage of the various tests and read into your mind. Get a clear and vivid picture of your psyche, analyse it and make necessary amendments as suggested. If you follow the advice given until it becomes a habit, you not only will be leaving procrastination far behind but also end up improving upon your personality and have a better mental health.

—Dr. Amit Abraham

Contents

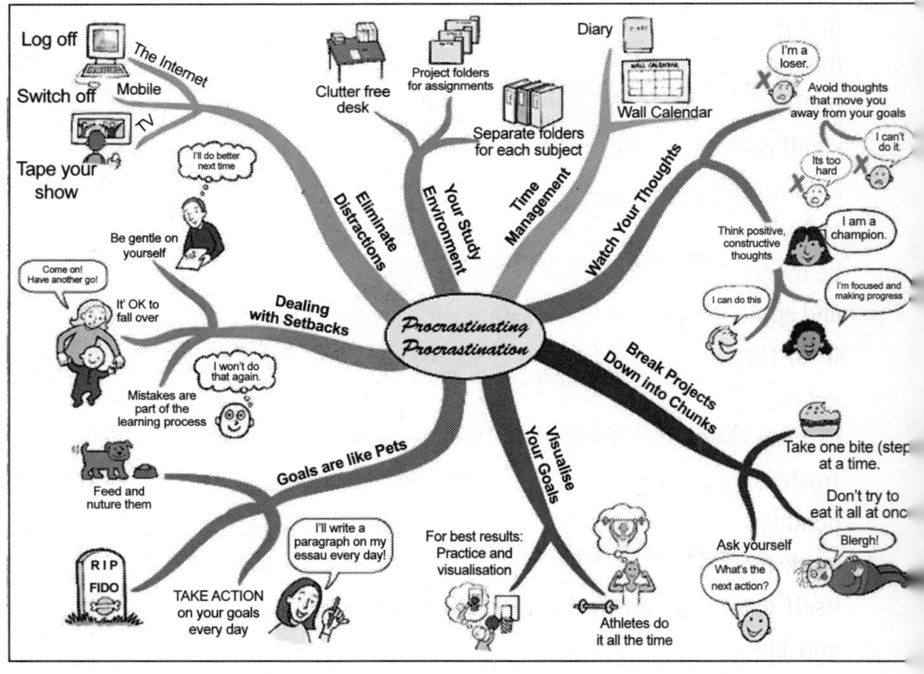

Procrastinating Procrastination
Eliminate Distractions
The Internet
Log off
Mobile
Switch off
TV
Tape your show
Your Study Environment
Clutter free desk
Project folders for assignments
Separate folders for each subject
Time Management
Diary
Wall Calendar
Watch Your Thoughts
I'm a loser.
Avoid thoughts that move you away from your goals
I can't do it.
Its too hard
Think positive, constructive thoughts
I am a champion.
I'm focused and making progress
I can do this
Break Projects Down into Chunks
Take one bite (step
at a time.
Don't try to
eat it all at onc
Blergh!
Ask yourself
What's the next action?
Visualise Your Goals
For best results: Practice and visualisation
Athletes do it all the time
Goals are like Pets
Feed and nuture them
RIP
FIDO
TAKE ACTION on your goals every day
I'll write a paragraph on my essau every day!
Dealing with Setbacks
I'll do better next time
Be gentle on yourself
Come on! Have another go!
It' OK to fall over
I won't do that again.
Mistakes are part of the learning process

Introduction

"How soon 'not now' becomes 'never'."

I have been planning to write this book since the last three years but have been finding some excuse or the other to avoid writing it. Looking back in retrospection I can list a thousand reasons for this procrastinating behaviour of mine and all seem very valid and justifiable to me. I recall when I was studying in school I had pasted a small poster in front of my study table which in Hindi read as – '*Aaj ka kaam kal par chhoro, kal kaam ka rate zyada milega*' – leave today's work for tomorrow as tomorrow the wages for the same will be more! To some extent it is true in the case of my book but not true and applicable to many other works which we all keep procrastinating from time to time. Many of you must have had the experience of getting your work done through government offices and all you get to hear every time is that the work will be done tomorrow. How frustrating it becomes when some other person keeps your work pending. On the other hand, when you keep yours or someone else's work pending it is such a relief. Thus, a procrastinating attitude in itself leads to a bundle of contradictory feelings. It sounds good for you but bad for others. Procrastination may appear good for those who indulge in it but it is only a temporary feeling because what needs to be done must be done – you cannot avoid it forever. This is where the problems begin and procrastinators become victims of their own procrastination.

However, it is not true that people only procrastinate things which they do not like to do or dread to do. I am a psychologist and I also do counselling columns for magazines and newspapers since the last many years. Many readers have shared their problems about their love and love life and what appears to be the most common problem is that of proposing to the one they love. Some ask me if they should propose to the person they love while others express their fear that if they wait for the correct moment to propose then someone else could beat them in proposing. Still others fear the thought of being rejected. Some are even very daring and want to propose to someone they have only seen but do not know personally. I now see all these acts relating with procrastination in some manner or the other. In these acts I see reasons of procrastination – seeking approval for the act, fear of rejection, and finally there are those who procrastinate love itself and need to just go ahead and express their feelings of the same. Similarly, there are cases of procrastination where marriage is concerned. There are those who delay in saying "I do" and tend to live happily ever after and there are others who readily or hastily say "I do" and then they themselves find out who lived happily thereafter. So procrastination is not only associated with what we want to avoid but at times also associated with what we want to achieve. Thus, procrastination at times becomes the fear of success. People procrastinate because they are afraid of success which they know will result if they move ahead now. Because success is heavy, it carries a responsibility with it, it is much easier to procrastinate and live on the *'someday I will'* philosophy.

As I have said above, I was procrastinating writing this book on Procrastination but I was not procrastinating working on the same. In the last three years I have been deeply engrossed in reviewing literature related to procrastination and conducted a few research studies myself. In fact, my procrastination should show more fruitful results. It is as such also important to differentiate between fruitful and fruitless procrastination. If you are procrastinating for a valid reason and this behaviour of yours is not directly affecting your life or has any negative effect on anyone else, then it can be termed as fruitful, provided that when you accomplish that procrastinated task, it should have added benefits for one and all. When procrastination is negatively affecting self or others then it is fruitless and harmful as well.

In today's lifestyle we all indulge in procrastinating some work or the other. Newly married couples procrastinate planning a family because they are too busy either making their careers or setting up house. Many students procrastinate studying and wait for the final date-sheet to be declared. Employees procrastinate various works which may not be to their liking or have no incentives. Children procrastinate many things because they are either addicted to television viewing or overburdened with their homework. At times we all have procrastinated indulging even in activities we like because other things merit priority which demand our time and attention. The list of procrastinations is endless but what is common is that there is a reason behind every act of procrastination – justifiable or not, but surely harmful to the procrastinator in the long run because procrastination is one of the most common and deadliest underlying causes of psychological problems and its toll on success and happiness is heavy.

Why Do We Procrastinate?

We all sorely complain of running short of time, and yet have much more time than we know how to spend it. Our lives are either spent in doing nothing at all, or in doing nothing to the purpose, or in doing nothing that we ought to do. We always complain that our days are few but act as though there is no end to consider. The truth is that we live our lives putting off all that can be put off – WHY!!!

On a scientific note, procrastination as viewed by mental health professionals is behaviour which is characterized by the deferment of actions or tasks to a later time. Psychologists often cite procrastination as a mechanism for coping with the anxiety associated with starting or completing any task or decision. Scientifically, procrastination is defined as "postponing the completion of a task to the point of feeling uncomfortable about one's delay". Some have also labelled procrastination as a "self-defeating" behaviour, even proposing intervention steps, as if procrastination were an illness. Some have tried to promote the positive side of procrastination as well, as according to them procrastination showed healthy benefits, including superior quality of work brought on by the pressure of an impending deadline. However, this positive side has very limited and short-lived benefits and also gives rise to more psychological problems.

Many reasons, singly or in combination lead us to procrastinate. Every individual is different from the other as far as the psychological pattern is concerned and thereby their reactions to similar situations and circumstances also vary. Various distractions and incompetencies that can cause procrastination, include, but which are not limited to the same are: **Addiction, Anxiety and fear, Arrogance, Pride, Aversion, Bad habits, Discouragement, Disorganization, Distraction, Family problems, Fear of failure, Feeling overwhelmed, Frustration, Ill-conceived goals and Unconscious motives, Indecision, Lack of awareness, Lack of morals, Lack of time management skills, Low ambition, Low frustration tolerance, Low self-esteem, Low tolerance to stress, Objective conflict, Paranoia, Perception of difficulty, Poor attitude, Poor self-control skills, Poor study skills, Rebellion, Resentment, Self-centredness, Self-deception, Uncertainty.**

Some Basic Reasons Behind Procrastinating

Some basic reasons are associated with signs of procrastinating behaviour. It will be good that before you proceed further in this book you check out which reason/s apply to you.

Skill deficit: This is one of the most basic reasons found in mostly all procrastinators. They simply put their hands up expressing helplessness. Since they lack skills required for performing the task they avoid doing so. So if you have been procrastinating doing or accomplishing tasks ensure if lack of skill is the reason for the same or not.

Lack of interest: It is a psychologically well accepted fact that we do not pay attention to things which are of no interest to us. Then how can we do or accomplish tasks which we are not interested in? Normal individuals make conscious efforts to attend to and accomplish even those tasks which don't hold their interests knowing very well their importance. Procrastinators on the other hand undervalue the importance of such tasks and refuse to attend to them stating that they are boring to do. So next time, when you find a task boring, or your natural interests are not stimulated towards that task, one solution to procrastinating would be to just do that task. This will give you more guilt-free time to do those things that are more interesting to you at a later time.

Lack of motivation: A life without motive is virtually a life without purpose. Motivation is a very important factor which determines one's behaviour. If one does not have the required need to fulfill something there will be no driving force. No driving force means no motivation. Procrastinators procrastinate because they do not feel the need to accomplish tasks. They simply lack motivation. Even if others try to motivate them they fail since the need is missing. This need cannot be created. It has to be self-generated. The best way to work this out is to begin working on the task and get motivated while doing it. Often just taking the first step, regardless of how small, can serve as an encouragement for further action.

Fear of failure: We all have so many fears deep within us but we do not let them take control over our lives. In fact, we control ourselves by overcoming the fears. Procrastinators, on the other hand, let these fears dominate their lives. The most dominating being the fear of failure. They believe that even if they try hard they will fail. They evaluate their fear as being worse than not accomplishing the required task. They begin to rationalize that if they give their best and yet fail, then it will be worse than not accomplishing the task at all. In the latter case, they can at least find solace in the fact that they did not try at all. If you are in the habit of procrastinating works because of the fear of failure, then remember that unless you give your very best, you will not find out what your true potentials are. May be, your actual personality is far better and more capable than the one you imagine to be.

Fear of success: This is another basic reason why individuals indulge in procrastination. Such individuals procrastinate because they fear the consequences of their achievement. They fear that if they perform well then the next time more will be expected out of them. Another reason associated with this is that such people shy away from being projected in the limelight preferring to stay in the background. This type of **task avoidance** may be the outcome of an internal identity conflict. When self-worth gets linked with the level of achievement then the question arises about how much one must do to be good enough. Each success only sets the stage for the next bigger challenge. It opens the door to greater and greater expectations from others. In such a situation people may become afraid of losing their identity and perhaps no longer be able to claim their successes as their own. Inaction or procrastination may be the outward expression of this feeling of being lost. In other words, procrastination may be attributed to how you could cope with the pressures you feel, to constantly try to be good enough. So, next time, when you fear success, just overrule the fear of consequences and go all out and achieve it. If you succeed, you are a winner but if you procrastinate, you not only lose, you get lost – lost in a world where actions matter the most.

Rebellion and resistance: Procrastination can be seen as a form of a rebellion or resistance towards authority as perhaps, reminiscent of an authoritarian parent. Incessantly being told what to do and being criticized or punished for not meeting the expectations, can be the ground for procrastination. Delaying tactics can be a form of rebellion against imposed schedules, standards, and expectations. Procrastination in this instance is the acting out of a power struggle, usually not on a conscious level. Rebellion and resistance are retaliatory actions; thus, the control of your behaviour rests with whatever or whomever you are rebelling against or resisting. If you are rebelling against your parents, then they have a great deal of control in your life, probably more than you really are ready to accept. Decide what you want because your life need not play to someone else's need.

Now if you are reading this book and have been indulging in procrastination, you may be getting an idea what makes you procrastinate. This book will help in educating you in detail about procrastination from a psychological view-point and try finding out the causes for your procrastinating behaviour. It will further help you in learning how to procrastinate procrastination because you need to know the true value of time; snatch, seize, and enjoy every moment of it. There should be no idleness, no delay, no procrastination and one should never put off till tomorrow what can be done today.

I'VE DONE NOTHING PRODUCTIVE
ALL DAY

1

Are You A Procrastinator?

"A year from now you may wish that you had started today."

Are you a procrastinator? Yes we all are but it is the degree of procrastination by each individual which distinguishes its severity. It thus becomes important to know right in the beginning if your level of procrastination is normal or a matter for concern. I will now put you through a simple questionnaire to measure your level of procrastination and thereafter help you understand and interpret the scores.

Procrastination Scale

Below are given statements which may/may not describe you. For each statement, decide whether the statement is characteristic or uncharacteristic of you, using the 5-point scale given below. Note that the 3 on the scale is Neutral (undecided) – the statement is neither characteristic nor uncharacteristic of you. Kindly express yourself in terms of your agreement or disagreement with the given characteristic in the statement. On the line next to the statement please write the number of the 5-point scale on the basis of your agreement/disagreement. Remember to be honest with your ratings.

5-POINT SCALE				
Strongly Disagree •	Disagree •	Undecided •	Agree •	Strongly Agree
1	2	3	4	5

1. I often find myself performing tasks that I had intended to do days before. ☐

2. I usually find reasons for not acting immediately on a difficult assignment. ☐
3. I find myself waiting for inspirations before becoming involved on most important study or work tasks. ☐
4. I know what I have to do but frequently find that I have done something else instead. ☐
5. When I am finished with a library book, I do not return it right away but wait for the date it is due. ☐
6. I carry my books and work assignments with me to various places but do not open them. ☐
7. When it is time to get up in the morning, I most often don't get right out of bed. ☐
8. I work best at the last minute, when the pressure is really on. ☐
9. A letter/e-mail may sit for days before I reply to it. ☐
10. There are too many interruptions that interfere with accomplishing my top priorities. ☐
11. I generally do not return missed phone calls promptly. ☐
12. I avoid forthright answers when pressed for an unpleasant decision. ☐
13. Even with jobs that require little else except sitting down and doing them, I find, they seldom get done. ☐
14. I take half measures which will avoid or delay unpleasant or difficult action. ☐
15. I usually don't make decisions as soon as possible. ☐
16. I have been too tired, nervous, or upset to do the difficult task that faces me. ☐
17. I generally delay before starting on work I have to do. ☐

18. I like to get my room/office in good order before starting a difficult study/task. ☐

19. I usually have to rush to complete a task on time. ☐

20. I do not do assignments until just before they are to be handed in. ☐

21. When preparing to go out, I am caught having to do something at the last minute. ☐

22. In preparing for some deadline, I often waste time by doing other things. ☐

23. I take my own sweet time to leave for an appointment. ☐

24. I usually do not start an assignment shortly after it is assigned. ☐

25. I rarely have a task finished on time. ☐

26. I always seem to end up shopping for birthday or festival gifts at the last minute. ☐

27. I usually buy even an essential item at the last minute. ☐

28. I rarely accomplish all the things I plan to do in a day. ☐

29. I am continually saying, "I'll do it tomorrow." ☐

30. I rarely take care of all the tasks I have to do before I settle down and relax for the evening. ☐

Total ☐

Scoring and Interpretation

After you have rated all the statements, add up the ratings. This will give you your total score on the measure of procrastination. If your scores are in the range of 110 – 150, it indicates high procrastination; 71 – 109 average procrastination; 30 – 70 low procrastination.

Now having obtained your measure on procrastination it is time that you take a look at the characteristic traits that procrastinators possess. It is not necessary that each of the mentioned traits is present in a procrastinator but even if a few are present the person has a tendency towards procrastinating.

Characteristic Traits of Procrastinators

The characteristics mentioned below are those which would match or resonate with just about anyone in our urban/western society. They are more a sign of the times than a useful diagnosis.

1. Procrastinators disappoint other people and themselves by not living up to their promises. For them this disappointing nature is a way of life.
2. Procrastinators, on a regular basis, seek excitement and attract attention of other people by their passive aggressive behaviour. Their excitement comes from not knowing how the person they have "wronged" will react when they see him/her again.
3. Procrastinators, by default, constantly place other people in a position of power over themselves.
4. Procrastinators project themselves as nice but indifferent individuals.
5. Procrastinators hate to be depended upon for any work.
6. Procrastinators seldom show up on time for appointments.
7. Procrastinators regularly procrastinate greatly over the things they have to do.
8. Procrastinators keep pending any decision which they have to make and thus with the course of time their decisions are made for them by the process of indecision – this is life's inevitable way of making the decisions for them and they have to accept it that way, irrespective of their liking or dislike of the same.
9. Procrastinators tend to avoid committed relationships. They generally get married at a late age or avoid getting married at all. They also delay in breaking off relationships which have soured.

10. Procrastinators indulge a lot in daydreaming or switching to other less important tasks. In this process they tend to avoid concentrating on projects that are at hand.

If your score was high on the procrastination measure you may have been able to identify with some or all of the characteristics which are present within you which make you a procrastinator. Further on, in this book I will educate you one by one with the various psychological and general causes of procrastination and those problems which can arise due to procrastination or, on the contrary, give rise to procrastination as well. I will also help you identify these causes and suggest corrective measures in helping you to procrastinate procrastination.

2

Some Facts About Procrastination

"Procrastination is also a subtle act of corruption – it corrupts valuable time."

Before I help you make an assessment about your traits in relation to procrastination it is important that I educate you with some more interesting facts about procrastination. It is important for you to familiarize yourself with these facts since upon these will be based the various measures of procrastinating behaviour and their assessment and thereafter remedial measures for procrastinating such a behavioural attitude.

Procrastination is like a grave in which opportunity is buried. Opportunities are generally seen and linked with making good use of the resources and bringing to exercise full potentials for achieving success in the future. Generally success has a two-dimensional picture – either its achievement, or a failure to achieve. Procrastination makes this picture multi-dimensional by adding more perspectives. It does not lead even to a failure to achieve because it jeopardizes the entire mechanism and buries alive what has been dead since long – the desire to achieve and the desire to succeed. Procrastinators sabotage themselves by digging their own grave. They not only create obstacles in their own path but intentionally choose such paths which hamper their productive output and negatively deter growth. Procrastination is hands down their favourite mode for self-sabotage.

We find that approximately twenty five percent of people identify themselves as very high procrastinators. Such people choose procrastination as their way of life, it is their style – they are always aspiring to live a new life, but never find time to set about it. This type of lifestyle is surely maladaptive and it cuts across all domains of their life. They don't pay their bills on time. They miss opportunities for investing money on time. They don't cash gift vouchers or deposit cheques on time. They file their tax returns late. They wait for the last moment to do most of the things.

A Peep into a Procrastinator's Psyche

1. ***Procrastinators have a profound problem of self-regulation:*** Self-regulation is an integrated learning process, consisting of the development of a set of constructive behaviours that affect one's learning. These processes are planned and adopted to support the pursuit of personal goals in changing learning environments. Recent research has suggested that the way people regulate their behaviour can have powerful effects on outcomes such as curiosity, persistence, learning, performance, effect, and self-esteem. Self-regulation implies the way individuals make use of internal and external cues to determine when to initiate, when to maintain, and when to terminate their goal-directed actions. Procrastination is seen as a failure in self-regulation.
2. ***Procrastinators procrastinating behaviour is conditioned:*** Procrastination is many a times a conditioned response which is acquired in the process of development and growth. It is the response which a child acquires when constantly confronting with authoritarian parenting styles. It is closely linked with self-regulatory behaviour as well. When parents are very harsh upon their children and exercise full control over them, they unknowingly handicap their children in their ability to regulate themselves. In such cases the child can also begin to use procrastination as a weapon for rebellion – delaying what is expected of him by his parents. This procrastinating attitude

of the child is also many a times reinforced by his peer group because they accept it without much fuss.

3. ***Procrastinators deceive themselves:*** "I am going to stop putting things off starting tomorrow." This is the biggest lie which a procrastinator tells himself because the very next day the same sentence will be uttered and tomorrow never comes. Procrastinators deceivingly also protect their sense of self-esteem by undermining the importance of tasks which they want to keep pending. Many procrastinators deceive themselves by creating an impression that they are more creative when they do tasks at the last moment – haste always makes waste. Research findings have shown that some people who in the past have enjoyed the buzz of adrenaline they gained from working under pressure, in the future they intentionally put off work in order to feel the tension of working close to a deadline. Such a practice can only be regarded as negative if the tendency to do this becomes addictive and the results gained from this approach to work are consistently poor.

4. ***Procrastinators focus their attention on distractions:*** Procrastinators intentionally bring to the focus of their attention things which can distract them and thus help in avoiding doing the task they have at hand. The stronger the attraction, the greater is the risk of distraction and stronger the procrastinating behaviour. This strategy is adopted by them for bringing themselves to a state of emotional equilibrium by neutralizing their fear of failure in the task at hand.

5. ***Procrastinators are impulsive people:*** Research has shown that individuals who are in the habit of procrastinating are generally very impulsive. This is so because they are more engrossed with the desires of the moment and pay little heed to those of the future. The engrossment with the present desires drives them to focus their attention upon immediate concerns

and immediate gratification. According to Freudian psychology such individuals are governed by the pleasure principle of the id – instantaneous gratification without concern for reality.

6. ***Procrastinators tend to avoid tasks they evaluate as unpleasant:*** At times procrastination is linked to avoidance of an unpleasant task. An individual may well have the ability, but not the inclination, to pursue a particular task that holds little interest for him/her. The inclination to do this is in proportion to the importance of the task to overall success and failure on a course. So if a task is not vital to the overall result, the more likelihood that procrastination will occur. In this situation, both, the incentives and rewards are weak.
7. ***Procrastinators generally suffer from mood related disorders:*** Procrastination in many cases is related with 'mood', or in some cases, depression – which is a more serious condition. In relation to mood, a typical response might be "I'm just not in the mood now, but will be later". This happens to us all, but becomes a problem if it becomes a regular attitude to any situation and disregards other life factors that you need to address. Depression, however, is a more significant issue, as this condition can physically lower one's interest and response to any activity.
8. ***Procrastinators are poor at time management:*** This is the most likely explanation for procrastination in an academic setting, particularly with students who are returning to education after a fairly lengthy break. They may use a mental benchmark for measuring the time that served them well during the holidays – but one that proves unsatisfactory to gauge the time needed to complete academic tasks. They consequently underestimate the time it takes to complete academic tasks, and defer starting work because of this lack of contextual time management experience.

9. ***Procrastinators generally have a high level of anxiety:*** Sometimes people with anxiety issues, or even generalized anxiety disorder, have problems with procrastination. Three major sources for this are: perfectionism, worry about results, and low self-efficacy.
10. ***Procrastinators tend to be perfectionists:*** Many times, people with anxiety also struggle with some degree of perfectionism. Worrying that everything needs to be perfect to be valuable and worthwhile, can leave one paralyzed with inaction.
11. ***Procrastinators worry about the outcomes:*** Another source of procrastination is worrying about what will happen after the event or work is completed. Sometimes we remain in a state of inaction as a means to avoid the results. The longer such people put off potentially stressful results, the longer they have to put up with a state of uncertainty and feel on tenterhooks, which is a huge source of anxiety itself.
12. ***Procrastinators have low self-efficacy:*** Self-efficacy is your belief in your ability to do something. Many times people procrastinate because they fear that they cannot do something well enough or because they do not know where to begin. Such people struggle to find out where to begin and finally end up never beginning.
13. ***Procrastinators may have physiological defects:*** Research on the physiological roots of procrastination mostly surrounds the role of the pre-frontal cortex. This area of the brain is responsible for executive brain functions, such as planning, impulse control, attention, and acts as a filter by decreasing distracting stimuli from other brain regions. Damage or low activation in this area can reduce an individual's ability to filter out distracting stimuli, ultimately resulting in poorer organization, a loss of attention and increased procrastination. This is similar to the prefrontal

lobe's role in attention-deficit hyperactivity disorder (ADHD), where under-activation is common.

Major Factors That Can Impact On Individual Responses to Task Procrastination

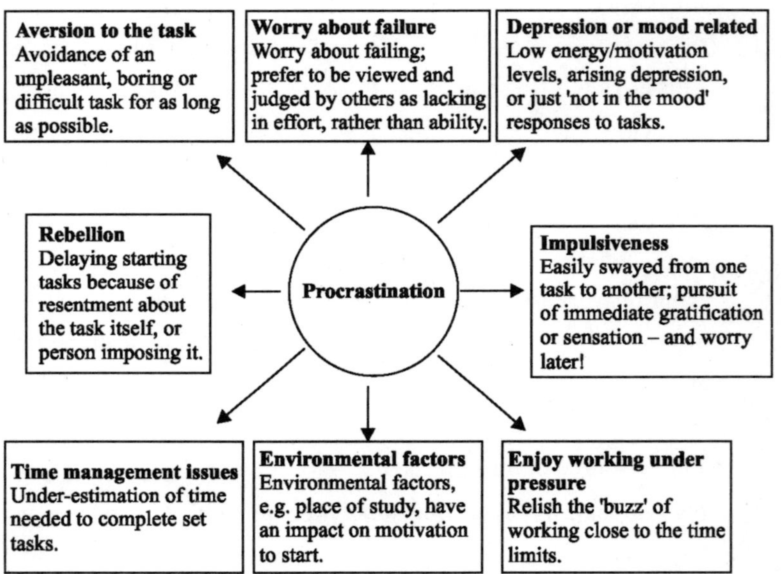

The Effects of Procrastinating

All of us procrastinate some task or the other but it does not imply that we are all procrastinators. Usually we are involved with multiple tasks and thus tend to procrastinate one work to attend to another. Our decision of procrastinating that specific task is based upon the priority it holds over other tasks. Thus, this type of procrastinating does not carry negativity. It becomes negative only when we indefinitely and intentionally keep required tasks pending and find reasons for not doing the same.

Procrastination affects every aspect of our lives. Some of the effects are positive while others are negative.

Positive Effects of Procrastination

Procrastination has largely been viewed as the cause of negative outcomes. However, on the basis of some recent researches done by psychologists they have been able to cite some advantages but these advantages are situation and circumstance specific. Many individuals who indulge in procrastination have lower levels of stress when they are required to begin with a task as compared to non-procrastinators. Procrastinators also seem to be more physically healthy than those who do not procrastinate their work. This is so because, at the beginning of the task, procrastinators are care-free as against those who start work immediately. Increased levels of stress and health problems begin right away for non-procrastinators. Therefore, procrastinators retain good health as long as the deadline is not near. Procrastinators also claim that an imposed deadline makes them more efficient and more motivated to do well.

However, don't be too happy if you are a procrastinator because this positivity is short-lived and gives rise to many physical and psychological problems in the long run. Avoid delays: Procrastination always does more harm than benefit.

Negative Effects

Short-term benefits have long-term costs. Procrastination is correlated with several health problems. Depression, vulnerable self-esteem and anxiety are related to those who procrastinate. Anxiety levels are especially high for procrastinators when they are to ultimately finish the task, and these same individuals feel maximum relief once they somehow finish the task. While procrastinators' stress level and health are good at the beginning of an assignment, problems arise as the deadline approaches. Setbacks do the most damage when one is starting a task late, as compared to the early starter who has more than enough time to deal with the task and continue as planned. The output of a task of a procrastinator is also not good even if he manages to finish the work. Procrastinators produce inferior work, contrary to beliefs that the best work is done under pressure. Researchers have suggested that possibly the ones who procrastinate have less intelligence but this has been contradicted by other studies.

Relation of Procrastination With Psychological Disorders

Procrastination also has a complex relationship with other psychological disorders. It relates to different systems of diseases and it seems to play a different role in each type of disease. Although, it is not these syndromes per se that correlate with procrastination, but a synergistic combination of traits. I will very briefly educate you about those psychological disorders which procrastination relates to. All relations mentioned are based upon various research studies.

Procrastination is related to Schizophrenia: Smoke psychologists, based upon their individual research studies, are of the opinion that schizophrenia and its parameters are unrelated to procrastination. However, on the other hand some also argue against this notion. For them schizophrenia does relate with procrastination. Their assumption is based upon the logical fact that schizophrenics often cannot accept their own successes and therefore use methods to delay progress – a characteristic trait of procrastinators.

Personality disorders are positively related to procrastination: Histrionic, narcissistic and borderline antisocial personality disorders are all correlated with procrastination. All these syndromes have a common variable of a lack of conscientiousness and impulsiveness which are characteristic traits found in procrastinators.

Disorders which are characterized by anxiety or fear are strongly related to procrastination: The need for procrastinators to perfectly control their environment and for perfectionism is correlated with psycho pathology. In particular, Passive personality disorders or emotionally unstable personality disorder uses procrastination, dawdling, stubbornness, intentional inefficiency and forgetfulness as a covert way of expressing aggression. Oppositional disorders are characterized by dependency, lack of self confidence, pessimism about the future, resentment to authority figures and procrastination. Symptoms of obsessive compulsive disorders include the traits of indecisiveness, doubt, perfectionism and inflexibility all related to procrastination of decisional tasks. Phobias are perhaps most directly related to procrastination and can result in task avoidance. However, often procrastinators have difficulty knowing what they are avoiding. Neuroticism has a curvilinear relationship to procrastination. It may however be only a specific subtype of neurotic symptoms i.e. sensitivity to rejection that is related to procrastination. Women in particular may suffer from anxiety which results in procrastination.

Procrastination as related with depression and other maladaptive behaviours: Procrastination is also a risk factor for depression and perhaps for other maladaptive behaviours. Whether procrastination is a risk factor or symptom of these syndromes is hard to determine as most studies have been co-relational, so causality cannot be determined. Procrastination may in fact be the beginning of a more serious disorder and can augment symptoms in vulnerable individuals. Often these patients put off treatment or have severe relapses. Procrastination can also result from neurological damage or deficiencies. However, procrastination is most importantly on its own, a maladaptive coping syndrome which needs to be treated seriously.

Is All Procrastination A Bad Thing?

So far there have been mostly negative connotations attached to the word 'procrastination', but as said before also, it is important to remember that not all deferment of action is bad. Sometimes procrastination is the wise and positive choice: in the case of war, for example, or any other situation when the outcome of an action is unpredictable and might even be harmful to others.

Procrastination can also be seen as a useful personal 'rebellion' against the unquestioning acceptance of task upon task that may unthinkingly be piled on us from all sides. It can be an opportunity to think about the range of tasks that we face, and whether they are all necessary, or really need to be accomplished in the time-frames set for us by others.

In many types of works some individuals deliberately leave work tasks to the last minute, arguing that the resulting pressures make them concentrate and give them the 'buzz' they need to produce consistent good work. If it has the desired effect, then that is fine. However, if deferment or avoidance of required tasks is not producing the desired result, and is leading to negative repercussions for you and for others, then procrastination of action to resolve the situation is unwise.

I have educated you with some facts related with procrastination. I believe now you are better equipped to help yourself or others in overcoming it. If you yourself are a procrastinator I am sure you will not be much happy with the negativity associated with procrastination and procrastinators. I assure you that as you progress reading this book and evaluating yourself on the various measures, you will begin to realize that procrastinating procrastination is going to benefit your physical and mental health and will help you in attaining success in your endeavours.

3

Types of Procrastination

"You know you are getting old when it takes too much effort to procrastinate."

The different types of procrastinations which are common, and recognized by researches are: the Behavioural Procrastination type, the Decisional Procrastination type, the Relaxed Procrastination type, the Intelligent Procrastination type, the Escapist Procrastination type, and the Afraid Procrastination type. However, it should be noted that there are many other ways in which types of procrastination has been classified both technically as well as in layman terms. What is important here is not the classification terminologies but knowing about procrastinating behaviour.

Usually procrastinators are a combination of different types, whether it is the Escapist Procrastinators who also consider themselves to be extremely intelligent, or it is the Decisional Procrastinators who feel that they should relax and unwind before making a decision. Once you determine the type of procrastination you suffer from; whether it is one kind or a little bit of each type, it is easier to overcome procrastination. Just do not put it off until it is too late.

If you are very high or high on procrastination let me run you through a test which will help you identify the type of procrastinator you are. Non-procrastinators can also take this test and recheck if they are not one of a type since the last measure of procrastination was not of a specific type but a general one.

This identification will help you better in knowing yourself besides overcoming procrastination. Kindly note that in the test below 'work' or 'task' means only those works or tasks which you do at home or on your job – it is not about anything impossible. Kindly try responding to all the questions with a 'Yes' or 'No'.

What Type of Procrastinator Are You?

Behavioural Procrastination Type (BPT)

1. I blame others for everything that goes wrong. Yes/No.
2. I do not take action to correct my mistakes. Yes/No.
3. I do not prepare before beginning important assignments. Yes/No.
4. Due to shortage of time many of my tasks are not accomplished properly. Yes/No.
5. I feel that my abilities are constantly being evaluated by others. Yes/No.

Total BPT : ☐

Decisional Procrastination Type (DPT)

1. I know which work I have to do first. Yes/No.
2. I have difficulty in deciding how to go about doing a task. Yes/No.
3. I finish off all my work at the last moment. Yes/No.
4. I spend a lot of time studying all the possible solutions available to accomplish a task at hand. Yes/No.
5. I want to do my entire task in a perfect manner. Yes/No.

Total DPT : ☐

Relaxed Procrastination Type (RPT)

1. I like to relax before beginning a task. Yes/No.
2. I feel that any task can be easily accomplished by me. Yes/No.
3. I like doing many things side-by-side. Yes/No.
4. I don't take tasks allotted to me very seriously. Yes/No.

5. I generally have a lot of work pending. Yes/No.

Total RPT: ☐

Intelligent Procrastination Type (IPT)

1. I find all kinds of work that I have to do very easy. Yes/No.
2. I readily understand the requirements of the works I have to do. Yes/No.
3. I am competent to do any work in a short period of time. Yes/No.
4. I devise various short-cut methods to accomplish my tasks. Yes/No.
5. I have problem managing my time while working on tasks. Yes/No.

Total IPT: ☐

Escapist Procrastination Type (EPT)

1. I spend a lot of time visualizing about the success of my present tasks. Yes/No.
2. I am not able to devote much time towards tasks I have to do. Yes/No.
3. I love relaxing and thinking a lot about the task I have to accomplish. Yes/No.
4. I can come up with many grandiose schemes guaranteeing sure success. Yes/No.
5. I feel that many tasks I have to do are barriers in my way to the achievement of my dreams. Yes/No.

Total EPT: ☐

Afraid Procrastination Type (APT)

1. I am many times unsure if I have the ability to accomplish tasks. Yes/No.
2. I need to bring down my stress level before beginning a task. Yes/No.
3. I feel afraid thinking about the outcome of my tasks. Yes/No.

4. I am rarely satisfied with the outcome of tasks I accomplish. Yes/No.
5. I face crisis when situations and circumstances become excessively demanding. Yes/No.

Total APT: ☐ **Grand Total:** ☐

Scoring and Interpretation

After you have marked your responses, give a point of 1 to every 'Yes' and a point of 0 to every 'No' you have marked. Then total up your scores for each type separately. The abbreviations are expanded below in the explanations of each type. If your score on any type is 3 or more then you fall into that/those category/categories. Kindly note if you have got a score of 2 or less in each type this does not mean that you are not a procrastinator but you are a mixed type. It is also not necessary that you fall into only one category type because there can be a little bit of each type also in a single procrastinator – excuses are all but too common. However, if you get a grand total (sum of all categories) in the range of 0 – 7 (with the condition that you have scored only 1 point each in any five categories and 2 points in any sixth category) you may not be a procrastinator but then may be a bluff master!!! You are the best judge of your procrastinating behaviour, so judge yourself honestly.

Furthermore, after you have identified the category or type of procrastinator you are, it is time that you know about that type and identify yourself. It is important that if you are a procrastinator you accept this fact which may taste like a bitter truth but will sweeten with your sincere efforts in procrastinating procrastination.

Procrastination Type

Behavioural Procrastination Type (BPT)

This type of procrastination is a self-sabotage strategy in which procrastinators shift the blame and thereby avoid taking the necessary action. For example, we come across many students who do not prepare well for their examinations and fare badly, who then blame their failure on the lack of time for preparation of their exams. This type of blame enables them to create the impression that they lacked effort more than ability.

Besides this, researchers have also put under this category those individuals who suffer from low self-esteem and self-doubt. Such individuals also have a strong concern relating to evaluation of their abilities by others. They view their self-worth as based on ability and thereby never accomplish tasks leaving no room for judgment of their abilities.

Prolonged procrastination and failure to perform adequately creates a cycle of self-defeating behaviour. This results in a downward spiral of self-esteem. Self-inflicted degradation and humiliation of this kind often translates into stress and (mental) health problems at some point.

Decisional Procrastination Type (DPT)

This type of procrastinator is good at recognizing the work that needs to be done but what hinders them is making decisions about the work. They strategically evade making decisions when they are confronted with conflicts or choices. Researchers have shown that individuals in this category of procrastination put off their decisions because they tend to fear committing errors. They also have an inclination towards perfectionism which acts as a catalyst in putting off things which require to be done. The strategy adopted by such procrastinators is very interesting and camouflaging. They involve themselves wholeheartedly in searching for more information about the various alternatives available before they come to any final decision, if they do make one at all.

The strategy adopted by decisional procrastinators leads them to a more confused state of mind and they end up falling prey to self-sabotage. With the many options that they explore and have at hand, they still end up with what is termed as optional paralysis. They create so many choices for themselves that they feel unable to choose, for fear of choosing an option that is less than perfect. Thus, this optional paralysis the entire functional machinery leading to no outputs.

Relaxed Procrastination Type (RPT)

The Relaxed Procrastinator does not take responsibility for the work that needs to be done seriously. They are perpetually lazy individuals who opt to be relaxed when it comes to doing the work that needs to be completed. When any work is to be accomplished such types of procrastinators compellingly feel that the work is very simple and can be accomplished within no time. This compelling feeling emboldens them to keep work pending till the eleventh hour. The relaxed procrastinators also show a tendency to indulge in other activities which they do not view negatively. Their preoccupation in other activities instead of the one at hand, reflects their non-serious attitude towards the importance of the task at hand and its accomplishment.

Intelligent Procrastination Type (IPT)

The Intelligent types of procrastinators believe everything comes easy to them, so they put off their work until the last minute. Their intelligence makes them lazy and their time management skills extremely suspect. They perpetually feel that any task which they need to accomplish is very simple to understand and execute, irrespective of its complexity. This very feeling compels them to postpone doing what needs to be done as they feel they can finish it in a very short time. Because of a false frame of time perception, when these people actually, if at all, get down to finishing the work at the last moment, they resort to short-cuts. They feel they are smart enough to simplify even the most complex projects. These simplified short-cuts in turn also end up in cutting short the work. Many important aspects of the work get missed out, thus hampering quality output.

Escapist Procrastination Type (EPT)

Daydreamers fall into the category of the Escapist Procrastinator. For them, in dreams reality does take shape but they never wake up to accomplish the same. They do have a lot of foresight but remain fixated at a point and forget to plan or work towards the final destination. Such people, like the relaxed type, also get addicted to seeking pleasure – they are under the domination of the pleasure principle of the id.. However, unlike the relaxed type, they do not view work in a negative manner. They are preoccupied most of the time thinking about possibilities. The Escapist Procrastinators spend too much time imagining flamboyant schemes but overlook existing realities. Their preoccupations with lucrative thoughts make them view their existing work as an obstacle to achieving their grand dreams. They surely know how to keep building castles in the air!

Afraid Procrastination Type (ADP)

Individuals coming under this category are those who believe that their capabilities are not good enough to complete the work. They consistently put off work until last minute. Such individuals face only crisis when situations and circumstances become excessively demanding and stressful. They begin to question their own capabilities and begin wondering if they could at all complete the demanding task at hand. Such individuals think they could work more efficiently if they relax before beginning a task. However, it is this relaxation which consumes time and also leads to building of pressure till they finally produce unsatisfactory output.

Some Quick Tips

It is very easy to diagnose procrastination but the difficulty begins when one has to work towards overcoming it. The only thing that can help you in overcoming your procrastination behaviour is your own determination to overcome it.

However, I am putting forth before you some quick tips related with what has been discussed above. Kindly note the tips do not follow any hierarchical order in relation to the above mentioned procrastination types.

1. ***You should realize the value or importance of the task which you are required to perform:*** In most of the tasks that are assigned to us or that we have to do, there is a goal to achieve. A simple example is, when you are feeling hungry and there is nobody to cook a meal for you. You have to make an effort to either cook food for yourself or have it from a restaurant. If you do not do so you will suffer from hunger pangs and your health also will be affected. In the same manner there are many tasks which need to be performed and their outcome is an attainment. It is important that you realize the importance or value of each outcome and thus put in the required effort to accomplish the tasks you are required to do or have to do.
2. ***Learn to be appreciative of all that you have to do:*** Unless and until you are appreciative of something, you cannot assign much value to it. It thus becomes important to look at the tasks that have to be done by you in a more positive manner. You may not like to do many routine tasks just because they do not interest you. There is a very old example of a glass holding water to half its capacity. I am using such an expression because it is up to the perceiver to evaluate if the glass is half empty or half full. If we perceive it as half empty we are not being appreciative – it is a negative thought. On the other hand if we perceive it as half full we are being appreciative and giving positive value to its content. The same applies with a task. Give positive value to it and it is your perception which can help you do it.

3. ***Have faith in your abilities:*** Usually people put off doing tasks because they do not trust their own potentials. I agree that some people are born great and on some, greatness is thrust upon. But then there are those also who achieve greatness. Such people work their way up the ladder one step at a time. They are laughed upon by others, evaluated in a negative manner but in the end they have the last laugh. They laugh best at the end because while on their way up they learned to trust their abilities and disregarded what others thought about them. It is very important what we think for ourselves. Opinions of others should not be stumbling blocks in achieving our goals.
4. ***Learn to make decisions and stick by them:*** Many times we procrastinate taking a decision about the task at hand. This stand of ours may be due to a conflict between two or more approaches. Many a times we also create conflicting options for ourselves – marriage or career first; this task or that task first; this mode or another mode and so on and so forth. It becomes very important that we evaluate a situation and weigh its pros and cons to arrive at a decision. We should keep our thoughts in check in relation to the problem and must be more focused. All these considerations will enable us take a decision and proceed with doing the task. Keep in mind that decision making is an important step towards ending procrastination.
5. ***Wake up – stay in touch with reality:*** If you want your dreams to turn into reality then wake up – Be realistic. Many procrastinators are in a habit of dreaming big but with their dreams reality ceases. One needs to be a visionary, plan in a concrete manner for the future but what is ultimate and of paramount importance, is 'the present'. There can be no future without the present. So put in your effort to accomplish the work at hand and achieve a firm goal.

6. ***Avoid creating self-stress for yourself:*** Many procrastinators by virtue of their laziness keep work pending for the eleventh hour. When the time comes to start the work they come under stress because of the shortage of time they have at their disposal. This stress is self created and can be easily avoided. Like I said above, planning of the task is important, a mental rehearsal of how it should be done helps further. Breaking the task down into its basic components is also a good option. It is all about scientific management – time and motion. I will discuss at length about stress and procrastination further on in this book.

This is not the end of suggestions for procrastinating procrastination but just the beginning. These suggestions are given here because if you wait for the moment when everything, absolutely everything is ready, you will never begin. I am going to help you stop putting things off starting tomorrow – so just begin now. Defer no time; delays have dangerous consequences. In the next chapters I will take you into the realms of procrastination psychology and educate you in depth about the major traits associated with procrastination. I will also suggest means and ways for procrastinating procrastination for each specific factor.

Quick Exercise

How many styles do you relate to?

Personality Type	Thinking Style	Speaking Style	Acting Style	Psychological Need For
Perfectionist	All-or-Nothing	I Should	Flawless	Control
Dreamer	Vague	I Wish	Passive	Being Special
Worrier	Indecisive	What If?	Cautious	Security
Crisis-Maker	Agitated	Dramatic	On the Edge	Attention
Defier	Oppositional	Why Should I	Rebellious	Non-Conformity
Pleaser	Compelled	Can't Say No!	Do-It-All	Acceptance

Throughout this book you will find mention or an explanation of these styles, so just remember the traits you have marked against each style. You can also always revert back if you don't feel too lazy to do so!

4

How Procrastination Affects One's Life

"Everything in human character goes to wreck, under the reign of procrastination, while prompt action gives to all things a corresponding and proportional life and energy."

Procrastination is the thief of time; year after year it steals and to the mercies of a moment leaves the vast concerns of an eternal state. At thirty, man suspects himself a fool; knows it at forty, and reforms his plan; at fifty chides his infamous delay, pushes his prudent purpose to resolve; in all the magnanimity of thought, resolves, and re-resolves, then dies anyway.

If you think that procrastination effects are only related with quality of work and output, you are highly mistaken. It effects our life in diverse spheres and many a time we are not even aware of this fact. A few of these aspects have already been dealt with so far with a lot of repetition. This repetition was required as each time they are talked about in a different context. Here again you may find it so but they need to be mentioned along with the other aspects.

Before I discuss these aspects it is important that I help you assess yourself on these aspects by a simple measure of how procrastination is affecting you. Kindly note that this measure applies, only if you have obtained a 'very high' or 'high' score on the procrastination measure. If you have not scored high on the procrastination measure and you obtain adverse results on this measure it means that there may be some other underlying psychological causes which are affecting your life and creating these problems. This book is only to address problems related with people who have a procrastinating behaviour and if you wish to know your cause you need to consult a counsellor or clinical psychologist.

Below are given statements and you are to respond in relation to their frequency of occurrence in your daily life. There is nothing right or wrong about the statements – they just express specific behaviour patterns. Kindly respond to all statements with full honesty.

Physical Experiences (PE)

1. When I have work at hand I get tensed. *Mostly/Sometimes/ Never.*
2. When I have to accomplish tasks my blood-pressure increases. *Mostly/Sometimes/Never.*
3. I experience an increase in oral sensitivity (mouth is highly sensitive) when there is a lot of work pending. *Mostly/ Sometimes/Never.*
4. I feel exhausted even before I begin to work. *Mostly/Sometimes/ Never.*
5. I easily get agitated when doing my work. *Mostly/Sometimes/ Never.*
6. I suffer from muscle aches as soon as I begin to do my work. *Mostly/Sometimes/Never.*
7. I have feelings of nausea while doing tasks I dislike. *Mostly/ Sometimes/Never.*
8. I experience restlessness whenever I have to meet deadlines. *Mostly/Sometimes/Never.*
9. I feel as if I am immobile in many work situations. *Mostly/ Sometimes/Never.*
10. I suffer from headaches while doing my works. *Mostly/ Sometimes/Never.*

Total PE: ☐

Mental Experiences (ME)

1. I am critical about all works that I do. *Mostly/Sometimes/Never.*
2. I don't have a high opinion about my own self. *Mostly/ Sometimes/Never.*

3. I don't have faith in my abilities/myself. *Mostly/Sometimes/Never.*
4. I keep thinking about not so relevant things. *Mostly/Sometimes/Never.*
5. I feel that I am unable to think at all. *Mostly/Sometimes/Never.*
6. I don't like following orders. *Mostly/Sometimes/Never.*
7. I want everything in perfect order. *Mostly/Sometimes/Never.*
8. I don't have many good things to say about myself. *Mostly/Sometimes/Never.*
9. I keep thinking about tasks which I don't want to do. *Mostly/Sometimes/Never.*
10. I have difficulty concentrating on my work. *Mostly/Sometimes/Never.*

Total ME: ☐

Emotional Experiences (EE)

1. I feel frustrated while working. *Mostly/Sometimes/Never.*
2. I feel irritated at others. *Mostly/Sometimes/Never.*
3. I suffer from feelings of guilt. *Mostly/Sometimes/Never.*
4. I avoid situations or activities because they cause me anxiety. *Mostly/Sometimes/Never.*
5. I fear that I will not be able to give satisfactory work outputs. *Mostly/Sometimes/Never.*
6. I worry about the accomplishment of works I have to do. *Mostly/Sometimes/Never.*
7. I get depressed not able to do my works. *Mostly/Sometimes/Never.*
8. I feel helpless while doing many tasks. *Mostly/Sometimes/Never.*
9. I envy those who get on with things. *Mostly/Sometimes/Never.*
10. I get angry at others while doing my work. *Mostly/Sometimes/Never.*

Total EE: ☐

Work and Career (W-C)

1. I am unable to make decisions. *Mostly/Sometimes/Never.*
2. I find working in a team very difficult. *Mostly/Sometimes/Never.*
3. I encounter minor accidents while executing my work. *Mostly/Sometimes/Never.*
4. I commit many mistakes while doing my work. *Mostly/Sometimes/Never.*
5. I shout at other people while in the process of doing my works. *Mostly/Sometimes/Never.*
6. I get exhausted while doing my works. *Mostly/Sometimes/Never.*
7. I miss out on golden chances for better career options. *Mostly/Sometimes/Never.*
8. I feel that my creativity has exhausted. *Mostly/Sometimes/Never.*
9. I put off doing things intentionally. *Mostly/Sometimes/Never.*
10. I think I have opted for the wrong career/course. *Mostly/Sometimes/Never.*

Total W-C: ☐

Relationships (WR)

1. My relationships with others seem like a burden to me. *Mostly/Sometimes/Never.*
2. I experience tension in maintaining my relationships. *Mostly/Sometimes/Never.*
3. I indulge in nagging people who are known to me. *Mostly/Sometimes/Never.*
4. I get frustrated when unable to maintain relationship. *Mostly/Sometimes/Never.*
5. I blame others for all the wrongs in my life. *Mostly/Sometimes/Never.*
6. I like being alone. *Mostly/Sometimes/Never.*

7. I don't feel the need for being loved. *Mostly/Sometimes/Never.*
8. I am not aware about what other people known to me are doing. *Mostly/Sometimes/Never.*
9. I don't like extending my help to anyone. *Mostly/Sometimes/Never.*
10. I feel that people known to me avoid me. *Mostly/Sometimes/Never.*

Total WR: ☐

Quality of Life (Q-O-L)

1. I experience a sense of spiritual emptiness. *Mostly/Sometimes/Never.*
2. I lack a sense of humour. *Mostly/Sometimes/Never.*
3. I don't laugh when I listen to jokes. *Mostly/Sometimes/Never.*
4. I feel that my sense of perspective has gone missing. *Mostly/Sometimes/Never.*
5. I feel that my ability to visualize a positive future has reduced. *Mostly/Sometimes/Never.*
6. I feel that it's too late for me to realize my dreams. *Mostly/Sometimes/Never.*
7. I feel that it's the end of the line for my growth. *Mostly/Sometimes/Never.*
8. I feel that I am going to stagnate where I am. *Mostly/Sometimes/Never.*
9. I feel that I am not as innovative as I used to be. *Mostly/Sometimes/Never.*
10. I think that there is no hope left within me. *Mostly/Sometimes/Never.*

Total Q-O-L: ☐

Scoring and Interpretation

After you have marked your responses assign a point of 2 to mostly; a point of 1 to Sometimes and a point of 0 to Never. After doing so total up your scores for each section. If you have obtained a score in the range of 21 – 14 the effect of procrastinating in that specific area is high (area abbreviations are expanded below with their explanations). If your score is in the range of 7 – 13 the effect of procrastination in that specific area is medium. If you have scored less than 7 then you need not worry – you appear to be well adjusted in the areas that you were tested upon.

Physical Experiences (PE)

Procrastination can lead one to a lot of physically unhealthy experiences. Any work at hand seems to build up tension within. This tension is more a conditioned response which has been associated with work that has been procrastinated in the past. Along with tension the blood pressure also is bound to increase. Sleep disturbances will also accompany these symptoms. The oral region becomes hypersensitive and you don't even like brushing teeth, leave aside aversion to many other ea-tables. With sleep disturbances fatigue is also normal to come. When work is pending one also gets into an agitated mood and for a procrastinator it is the norm. Feelings of restlessness are but too common – restless because nothing is happening. A procrastinator does not feel like moving around due to the feeling of being glued to the spot he is in. He has constant headaches, muscle aches, backaches and gives anxieties to others also by his procrastinating behaviour.

So you suffer so many physical discomforts just by procrastinating work routines. If you really want to avoid experiencing these emotions then my advice is that you begin addressing the same – it is your work and your health so take care of both on time. At least earn these physical experiences!

Mental Experiences (ME)

Procrastination not only affects your physical experiences but your mental ones as well. A procrastinator becomes self-critical and tends to adopt a critical outlook about everything and everyone. This critical tendency may be the outcome of either being criticized by others or a mode of putting blame on others for all mistakes. It can also be related with avoidance behaviour. The causes can be many but self-criticism is destructive and devastating for the procrastinator. You cannot appreciate yourself, or others. You begin to undervalue yourself and question your own abilities leading to low self-esteem. Your low self-esteem is also connected with your low self-belief. You do not believe in yourself thus losing whatever little confidence you have left in you. You suffer from obsessive thinking which hampers your focus on goals which you have to achieve. This obsessive thinking also gives rise to a sort of mental paralysis. You feel that your thinking has got jammed and the brain is simply not functioning. Weighed down with so many adverse emotions you begin to rebel against one and all. This rebellion is an indication of your very own inner turmoil which you are unable to resolve. And in spite of all this, even if you are left with the mental energy to act you look for perfection. There is nothing more perfect than perfect procrastination for a Perfectionist Procrastinator.

Emotional Experiences (EE)

There are many emotional experiences which a procrastinator relates with. These emotional experiences can be labelled as 'negative emotions'. They become overwhelming just when the procrastinator is to begin a task which he dislikes. These emotions are aptly called negative because there are mixed emotions in the turbulent wave of emotions that procrastinators report – fear, anxiety, frustration, guilt, shame, anger, irritability, worry, tearfulness, depression, sense of helplessness, and feeling of envy for others. The procrastinator, upon experiencing these emotions wants to get rid of them at the earliest and the quickest route is to avoid what brings about such emotions – no work and no negative emotions bring relief.

In wanting to return to a state of emotional equilibrium the procrastinator will begin to concentrate on immediate modes of attaining emotional stability and so will forego any activity that will lead to attainment of required future goals.

So if you are experiencing negative emotions, identify them and deal with them – they need your work outputs. Not escapism. This process will help you move one step up on the ladder towards attaining your goal – both procrastinating procrastination and your achievement as well.

Work and Career (W-C)

Procrastination is the arch rival to productivity. Procrastinating work and career matters is very damaging because you don't only get yourself in trouble, you can get colleagues and seniors in trouble as well if you aren't completing your assignments on time. At the end, however, the greatest pressure is on you, so you will take the impact of the stress and the consequences.

Although there are hundreds of reasons why individuals procrastinate and put off difficult tasks, one of the most common reasons why individuals procrastinate is because they are simply overwhelmed by a task which seems too large in scope to complete. Such individuals then find it difficult to make decisions. They don't feel comfortable while working with others and are prone to committing errors. They lose their temper easily and feel exhausted without adequate reasons. They are not satisfied with their job or career and miss out taking advantage of career growth opportunities because of their procrastinating tendency.

Each one of us has a lot of work to do every day and it is not possible that all work be finished on the same day. However, many individuals get tensed and this pressure can result in feelings of being overwhelmed which in turn leads to procrastination at work which can actually decrease productivity, if not properly managed.

So if your score is high on the work and career experiences, you need to follow this advice: Identify which tasks you put off and why? If lack of knowledge is keeping you from putting off doing something, get help. Break down each task into small manageable parts. Work on each part for a pre-set amount of time, i.e. ten minutes, and then stop. Take a break and then work on the next part. Reward yourself for completing a task. You should also organize your work area. Complete tasks you don't like doing, when your mind is clear. Finally, do not hesitate to ask for help if you don't understand how to do something.

Relationships (WR)

Relationships are crucial for all human beings. It is difficult to establish and maintain relationships but very easy to end them. Like tasks, relationships also require conscious efforts to make it last – it cannot be taken for granted. However, individuals who have a procrastinating tendency easily mess up relationships by simply not putting in the required effort to save it. For such individuals it appears like a Herculean task. It's like they are being forced to carry a burden. They experience tension, indulge in nagging their near and dear ones and people known to them. The thorny hand of frustration also clinches them when they find themselves unable to maintain relationships. Frustrated, they begin the blame game – blaming others for whatever goes wrong in their lives. They isolate themselves and don't feel the need for love, belonging and affection. This self isolation makes them insecure and they feel that people are avoiding them instead of the other way round.

If you want to remain mentally healthy and happy it is very important that you strive to maintain your relationships. Evading people and spoiling your relationships will affect every nook and corner of your life. Love, belonging and affection are basic needs which every human and animal as well, needs fulfillment of. So make conscious efforts to reach out to your loved ones.

Quality of Life (Q-O-L)

The quality of life of people who indulge in procrastination is also drastically affected. When one habitually procrastinates his work, his creative ability diminishes. He also experiences spiritual emptiness and his humor becomes "gallows laughter". He puts his laughter on silent mode not reacting heartily to jokes and satires. He loses his sense of perspective and thus fails to give proper directions to his life. There is also drastic reduction on his ability to visualize a positive future for himself and for those who matter for him. He begins to feel depressed with the thought that his life is passing by him and all his prospects look stunted.

So if you catch yourself procrastinating then beware! You may have to pay a very heavy price for the same. Your quality of life will deteriorate and you will lose control over yourself. If you indulge in procrastination, you will conclude that because a thing ought to be done, you can't do it! Just take a decision spontaneously because in that moment of decision, the best thing you can do is the right thing to do. The worst thing you can do is nothing. It is perfect that you do the best thing – act and don't bring the curtains down on the quality of your life.

Procrastination is a way for us to be satisfied with second-rate results; we can always tell ourselves we could have done a better job if only we had more time. If you're good at rationalizing, you can keep yourself feeling rather satisfied this way, but it is a clumsy satisfaction. You're whittling your expectations of yourself down lower and lower. One of the most tragic things about human nature is that all of us make the mistake to put off living. We are all dreaming of some magical rose garden over the horizon – instead of enjoying the roses blooming outside our windows today. The really happy people are those who have broken the chains of procrastination, those who find satisfaction in doing the job at hand. They are full of eagerness, zest, and productivity. You too can be! Don't procrastinate. Putting off an unpleasant task until tomorrow, simply gives you more time for your imagination to make a mountain out of a possible molehill, more time for anxiety to sap your self-confidence. Act now or it's never done.

How Procrastination Effects Our Life

1. Physical Experience

- Tension
- Raised blood-pressure
- Sleep difficulties
- Increased oral sensitivity
- Fatigue or ultra-active
- Agitation
- Nausea
- Restlessness
- Immobilisation
- Physical problems left unattended may worsen
- Headaches, muscle aches
- Increased use of stimulant

2. Work/Career

- Pre-occupation with the "thing" which is being put off can lead to reduced effectiveness in decision-making, reduced contribution to team working, increased likelihood of accidents, mistakes, outbursts and burn-out.
- Missed carrer opportunities
- Reduction in creative output

3. Emotional Experience

- Frustration
- Irritability
- Guilt
- Anxiety
- Fear
- Worry
- Tearfulness
- Anger
- Depression
- Sense of helplessness
- Envy of others who get on with things

4. Mental/Cognitive Experience

- Self-critical
- Low self-esteem
- Low self-belief
- Obsessive thinking
- Sense of thinking being "jammed"
- Rebelliousness
- Perfectionism

5. Quality of Life

- Diminished creativity
- Sense of spiritual emptiness
- Humour becomes "gallows laughter" or is lacking
- Sense of perspective is lost
- Ability to visualise a positive future is reduced
- Sense of "life passing you by" and or growth and hop both being stunted

6. Within Relationships

- Relationships become fraught and tense
- Nagging and frustration
- Blaming and accusation
- The person who is procrastinating may be so preoccupied they isolate themselves, thus becoming less aware of others, and less loving and giving
- People around someone procrastinating may feel helpless or feel they need to distance themselves,especially if something affecting health is involved.

❑❑❑

PERFECTIONISM IS THE MOTHER OF PROCRASTINATION

5

The Perfectionist Procrastinator

"It is not because things are difficult that we do not dare, it is because we want perfection which makes them difficult."

In psychology, perfectionism is a belief that perfection should be strived for. However it becomes pathological when this belief turns unhealthy due to the individual being obsessed with the idea that anything less than perfect will not be acceptable to him. This unreasonable obsessive thought patterns drives him to put in his very best and yet not be satisfied with the outputs. When perfectionism is used as an excuse for poor performance or to seek sympathy and affirmation from other people it can lead to self-deprecation. Finally it can also lead to procrastination, by evading work out of fear of not being able to achieve perfection. In the workplace, perfectionism is often marked by low productivity, as individuals spend time and energy on small irrelevant details of larger projects or mundane daily activities. In all instances it brings about nothing but adds imperfect problems for the individual.

Inculcation of Perfectionism

When perfectionism gives rise to a tendency to negatively evaluate outcomes and personal performance, or creates intense fear and brings about an avoidance of evaluation of one's abilities by others then it leads to procrastination. On a pathological level perfectionism can also be associated with an exaggerated social self-consciousness anxiety, and recurrent depression.

The need for perfectionism begins with upbringing. Speaking in psychological terms it is a result of an attempt on the part of the child to seek intimacy and gain approval from a distant or critical parent. In his effort to be perfect the child creates an idealized or perfect self, to replace or to hide the inadequate true self. The result of such an effort undermines the actual self. The perfect one then over-rides it giving birth to perfectionism. The dominance of the ideal self alters the child's personality. The child's personality may appear pleasing on the outside but from within it is critical or angry. The projected pleasing personality is a camouflage to conceal the true inadequate self for fear of rejection and replace an acceptance seeking personality. This is so adopted because the child wants to feel better from within by gaining approval and to bring in emotional supplies that are in short supply because of a critical internal environment. The original anger the child felt toward his parents which was internalized comes back to him as self criticism and makes it impossible to fully take in the approval from pleasing people. Finishing tasks then becomes a referendum for his adequacy. Now comes in the role of procrastination. It has two main purposes, first to avoid acceptance of inadequacy because the product will never be perfect enough and, second to evade self criticism when the outcome is less than perfect.

Dimensions of Perfectionism

Recently, perfectionism has been defined as multidimensional. It includes six factors: concern over mistakes, personal standards, parental expectations, parental criticism, doubts about actions, and organization. Perfectionists are highly concerned about their mistakes, have high personal standards, and favour extremely organized style. In addition, they are susceptible to parental criticism and expectations. Perfectionism is also divided into self-oriented perfectionism (i.e., demanding perfection of oneself), other-oriented perfectionism (i.e., demanding perfection of others) and socially prescribed perfectionism (i.e., perceiving that others are demanding perfection of oneself.). Self-oriented perfectionists adhere to strict standards while maintaining strong motivation to attain perfection and avoid failure; engage in stringent self-evaluation. Such perfectionists derive a sense of pleasure from their labours and efforts, which in turn enhances their self-esteem and motivation to succeed and eventually helps them to develop a sense of control over their environment. Self-oriented Perfectionists may then use their pleasure in their accomplishments as encouragement to continue and even improve their work. On the other hand Other-oriented Perfectionists set unrealistic standards for significant others (e.g., partners, children, co-workers) coupled with a stringent evaluation of others' performances. Socially-prescribed Perfectionists believe that others hold unrealistic expectations for their behaviour (and that they cannot live up to this); experience external pressure to be perfect, believe others evaluate them critically. Such perfectionists do not derive pleasure from their labours and efforts and tend to view their work as inadequate or inferior. Furthermore, they report experiencing external pressure and or coercion to accomplish tasks. Therefore, the maladaptive symptoms of the Socially Prescribed Perfectionist emerge not from an internally felt desire to be at their best, but more from a fear of failure and/or a desire to avoid embarrassment, humiliation and guilt.

Self-oriented Perfectionism is the intra-personal aspect of 'perfectionism' and 'Other-oriented Perfectionism' and 'Socially prescribed Perfectionism'. Research shows that self-oriented perfectionism has consequences on individual's psychological adjustment such as lower self-esteem, depression, anxiety, avoid-ant coping, fears of negative evaluation and so forth.

There are also two categories of perfectionism: Adaptive and Maladaptive Perfectionism. Adaptive Perfectionism embraces characteristics such as high personal standards, order and organization, and an unwillingness to procrastinate. While Maladaptive Perfectionism embraces excessive concern about mistakes and doubts about their actions, they are more likely to have critical parents who expect a lot from them, so they are more likely to procrastinate. Adaptive Perfectionism is significantly related with self-esteem, whereas Maladaptive Perfectionism is not significantly related with self-esteem. Therefore, Maladaptive Perfectionism is the negative form of perfectionism.

Maladaptive Perfectionism has been associated with psychological and physical problems such as depression, anxiety, substance abuse, migraines, chronic pain, suicidal ideation and eating disorders. On the other hand, Adaptive Perfectionism shows positive achievements and adjustment, high self-esteem, social adjustment, and positive vibrations, in general. It has been found that high achievers are more at risk of being Maladaptive Perfectionists than those who are not high achievers.

Relationship Between Perfectionism And Procrastination

Researches of several psychologists suggest that there is a link between procrastination and perfectionism. They claim that procrastinators place unrealistic demands on themselves. These studies reveal that procrastinators demonstrate many of the cognitive characteristics associated with perfectionism, including the tendency to endorse the importance of continual success. Both are also related to increased endorsement of irrational beliefs. They are also linked together based on the fact that procrastination and perfectionism are associated with excessive fear of failure. However, this relationship between perfectionism and procrastination is quite complex. This is so since the perfectionism construct is multidimensional and has both personal (i.e., high standards, over-concern with mistakes, doubts about actions, organization) and social components (i.e., high parental expectations, parental criticism). Whereas self-oriented perfectionism involves high standards and motivation for the self to attain perfection, in the case of Other-oriented Perfectionism the tendency is to expect others to be perfect. By definition, Other-oriented Perfectionists engage in various kinds of extra-punitive behaviour. In contrast, Socially prescribed Perfectionism is the perception that other people expect oneself to be perfect. Socially prescribed Perfectionism is associated with various kinds of negative adjustment, in part, due to the lack of control and exposure to criticism associated with imposed standards of perfection.

Researches done so far, have found a significant association between socially prescribed perfectionism and indices of procrastination. There is a positive association between procrastination and high parental expectations and high parental criticism. Lending support to this relationship other studies have found that procrastination on everyday tasks was associated with "Covert Negativism". Covert Negativism is conceptualized as the extent to which a task is perceived as an imposition and the person resents being forced to do the task. This is similar though not identical to socially-prescribed perfectionism, in which an individual perceives that other people are imposing unrealistic demands on the self.

Fears of failure and task aversion are two important components of procrastination. Studies reveal that there is a significant strong association between the fear of failure factor and all components of perfectionism except the organization factor of perfectionism. Similarly, the task aversion factor is found to be associated with all but the high personal standards component of perfectionism.

Now having understood about the complicated relationship between procrastination and perfectionism it is time for you to know if you are a perfectionist or not. Knowing this is important for you to understand about perfectionism in its totality and how it relates with procrastination in your case, if at all.

Are You A Perfectionist?

The measure of perfectionism is designed specifically to evaluate your perfectionism on six dimensions. It is very important that the dimensions of perfectionism also be identified for relating it with procrastination, based upon researches conducted in this area.

Read each statement carefully and assign the appropriate weight based upon its applicability to you. The weights to choose from are given below and to be assigned by you after each statement in the space provided thereafter. Remember that your honesty is very important.

Points

0 – Never.

1 – Sometimes.

2 – Most of the time.

3 – Always.

Concern over Mistakes (CM)

1. I fear the very thought of failure. ☐
2. If I make a mistake I feel upset. ☐
3. I feel as if I have failed in a task if someone does it better than me. ☐
4. For me even a failure in part is equal to complete failure. ☐
5. I never settle for being second best in anything. ☐
6. If I make a mistake I feel that others will look down upon me. ☐
7. I suffer from inferiority if I am unable to outperform others. ☐
8. I feel I will lose my respect if I always do not excel. ☐
9. I feel that I will be admired more by others if I commit lesser mistakes. ☐
10. If I fail at any task I feel that I am a failure as a person. ☐

Total CM: ☐

Doubts about Actions (D)

11. I feel that even if I do anything carefully it is not done properly. ☐
12. I doubt my ability to accomplish tasks. ☐

13. I have doubts about the simple everyday things I do. ☐
14. I lag behind in my work as I keep rechecking what I have done. ☐
15. I take a long time to do something correctly. ☐
16. I find it hard to believe I have done a thing correctly. ☐
17. I doubt that I take proper measures in doing tasks. ☐
18. I doubt the quality of my actions. ☐
19. I do my work very meticulously yet I am not sure it's being done perfectly. ☐
20. I doubt the actions I take while working. ☐

Total D: ☐

Parental Expectations (PE)

21. It is/was difficult for me to meet the high standards set by my parents for me. ☐
22. My parents expect/expected me to excel in all that I do/did. ☐
23. My family is/was appreciative only of outstanding performances. ☐
24. My parents expect/expected only excellence from me. ☐
25. The expectation of my parents for my future is/was higher than my own. ☐
26. There is/was a lot of pressure on me to do well in school. ☐
27. My parents expect/expected me to fulfil their dreams. ☐
28. I was/am expected to behave in a disciplined manner. ☐
29. My parents expect/expected me to achieve perfection in all that I do/did. ☐
30. My fear/feared punishment from my parents if I fail/failed to meet their expectations. ☐

Total PE: ☐

Parental Criticism (PC)

31. If I don't do/did things according to my parent's expectations I am/was punished. ☐

32. My mistakes are/were never understood by my parents. ☐
33. I never feel/felt that I can/could meet my parents' expectations. ☐
34. I never feel/felt like I can/could meet my parents' standards. ☐
35. My parents always criticize/criticized me. ☐
36. I am/was blamed for everything that goes/went wrong. ☐
37. My parents are/were never appreciative of whatever I do/did. ☐
38. My parents find/found fault in all that I do/did. ☐
39. I fear/feared if I do not/did not do things properly then I will/would be criticized by my parents. ☐
40. Fear of my parent's criticism makes/made me defer my works. ☐

Total PC: ☐

Personal Standards (PS)

41. If I don't set the highest standards for myself I feel that I will end up like a second-rate person. ☐
42. I need to be thoroughly competent in everything I do. ☐
43. Goals set by me for myself are higher as compared to those of others. ☐
44. While attaining a goal I am very good at focusing my efforts on the same. ☐
45. My goals are extremely high ones. ☐
46. In my comparison other people seem to accept lower standards than I do. ☐
47. I expect higher performance in my daily tasks than most people. ☐
48. I want to be the best. ☐
49. I do my work with utmost dedication. ☐
50. I compete with my own self to do better and better. ☐

Total PS: ☐

Organization (O)

51. I like to keep everything organized. ☐
52. I keep my rooms tidy. ☐
53. I hate those who are unorganized in their work. ☐
54. I keep back everything in its right place. ☐
55. Neatness is very important to me. ☐
56. I am an organized person. ☐
57. I keep my surroundings neat and tidy. ☐
58. Disorganization irritates me. ☐
59. I do my works in an organized manner. ☐
60. I feel that organized working is a key to success. ☐

Total O: ☐

Grand Total: ☐

Scoring

After you have assigned the weight to all the statements, total them up for each dimension and write it down in the space provided for the total. Thereafter total up the scores obtained for each dimension **except that of O.** This will give you your total score on perfectionism. Kindly note that the range of the scores in terms of level of perfectionism is the same for all the dimensions but the interpretations for each dimension as related with procrastination are different.

Sub-score range: If you have obtained a score in the range of 21 – 30 you have high level of perfectionism in that specific dimension; in the range of 11 – 20 it is medium and in the range of 0 - 10 it is negligible.

Total score range (CM + D + PE + PC + PS): If you have obtained a score in the range of 101 – 150 you have a high level of perfectionism; in the range of 51 – 100 it is medium and 0 – 50 it is negligible. (The O dimension has been excluded from the total scores because it has a very negligible effect on perfectionism and its score if included, may drastically influence the overall interpretation).

Interpretation

We will interpret each dimension of perfectionism separately, briefly associating it with procrastination based upon researches done in the past which have related it with procrastination.

Concern over mistakes (CM): Research has shown that there is a significant relationship between concern over mistakes and procrastination. Individuals who are highly concerned about committing mistakes tend to indulge in causing delay in doing things. This delay is due to the various types of irrational fears they have conditioned themselves with. Their fears are largely related with mistakes they might commit, fear of not being able to do better than others, fear of not doing an outstanding job, fear of being looked down upon in case output is less than the best, fear of feeling inferior if not able to outperform others, fear of losing respect, fear of losing the admiration of others, fear of being a total failure. All these different types of fears are the outcome of the tendency such individuals have towards perfectionism. They want to make no mistakes and want a perfect output but the biggest mistake they make is succumbing to such irrational fears leading to delays in output or procrastinating work indefinitely.

Doubts about actions (D): Research has also indicated a significant relationship between doubts about action and procrastination. Doubts about action is an absolute prerequisites for perfectionism and thereby procrastination. The problem that arises in such cases is, desire to be a perfectionist but not having the confidence in actions. Individuals who doubt their actions also have a low level of self-confidence. They doubt their ability to do anything carefully, to accomplish things they are doing and even when tasks are finished they doubt things have been done properly. Such doubting attitude drags such individuals to either delay in starting work or slackness while doing it. They check and recheck upon their work at each step and stage out of doubt if it is being done properly. Apart from other reasons one of the components of this doubt is their perfectionist attitude. To do things in a perfect manner they begin to doubt if it is being done perfectly. This doubt either compels them to procrastinate work or delay it due to the snail speed they work at.

Parental expectations (PE): Research has found that increased procrastination is associated with high parental expectations. This indicates that procrastination may be a response to the expectation that parents will respond to self-characteristics in a punishing manner. Parents generally have very high expectations from their children and do not evaluate the potential within their children to meet these expectations. All they ever want is that their child should excel and supersede all. This unrealistic expectation of the parents puts undue pressure upon the child. He in the beginning tries to work meretriciously trying to bring about perfection in all he does. However, in most such cases the child fails to live up-to parental expectations – he fails to bring about perfectionism in all that he does. To avoid pressure the child then begins to procrastinate his work using it as an escape mechanism. This tendency carries on forward into adulthood and his work output is drastically affected.

Parental criticism (PC): Parental criticism is also significantly related with procrastination. Perfectionists perceive that their parents are/were excessively critical. This critical attitude of the parents instils fear within the child and he strives for perfectionism to avoid being criticized. This striving soon becomes a habit which tends to interfere with work and its output. As the individual grows he begins to fear criticism in whatever he intends to do or does. To avoid criticism he attempts his work with perfection but then this very perfection becomes the reason for procrastination of work or delayed output.

Personal standards (PS): Perfectionists don't just set very high standards, but also place excessive importance on those standards for self-evaluation. However, though high personal standards are a dimension of perfectionism they do not necessarily significantly relate with procrastination. Setting high personal standards leads one to strive harder for the attainment of the goal. The problem arises when such individuals begin with the self-evaluation process – comparing themselves with others and self. This is where they bring in negative vibes. It is not always that they fare better than others or meet the standards they have set for themselves. Once they begin to fail on their very own measures, chances are high for procrastination to set in.

Organization (O): Being an organized worker is again a positive aspect of perfectionism. Organization brings in readiness and creates a desire to execute the work at hand. Thus, organization though being a dimension of perfectionism, does not significantly relate with procrastination. On the other hand it can act as a catalyst to work and work conditions. However, there sure is a catch in here. If one is obsessed with being highly organized and any sort of disorganization distracts him it is bound to interfere with work, its quality and overall output. Many a times, one may not feel like doing any work if things are not organized according to his taste. So obsession with organization can lead one to procrastinate.

Overcoming Perfectionism To Avoid Procrastinating

Having measured yourself on the perfectionism measure you must be now aware as to where you stand. If you are a procrastinator and your score on the perfectionism measure is above the normal range then you need to look deep within yourself. You need to take control of your life and not let perfectionism lead you to missing out on its finer aspects. Procrastinate Procrastinating Perfectionism! Just make your life perfect without looking for perfection into each and every thing and ultimately not achieving any results. Let go of your inner inhibitions and follow the following advice – just see how perfectly it will work in driving away both procrastination (if you have it) and perfectionism if you are high on it.

1. **Lead A Balanced Life:** Look back on the days when procrastination and/or perfectionism was not high on your agenda and see what is missing now as a Procrastinator and/or a Perfectionist. Has procrastination influenced by perfectionism rendered you less productive in your output? Has it taken away the recognition that you were earning for what you did? You were then not under any self-imposed pressure to achieve. Your life now has been devoid of new experiences and you have lost all the fun filled time you used to spend with family and friends… this list can go on but you make your own! Check out how unbalanced your life has become. The balance needs to be brought back. This balance in life will make you feel sufficiently positive and enhance your self-esteem by providing habits and thought patterns which in turn will make perfectionism a redundant need. Easier said than done! Ok, let's see how you will go about doing it.

   Take your pick and prioritize the things you have been missing in life since you became a staunch perfectionist (I am sure you were not born as one). These missing links in your life has deviated your path from normalcy. The enrichment you had has depleted over 'perfect time wasted imperfectly over perfecting the art of perfect perfectionism'. This has caused insecurities to develop within you (imagine what a depleted bank account can do). The more anxious, insecure and doubtful about your worth you feel, the more you are likely to place emphasis on those very elements on which you are already placing emphasis on – trying to be perfect! It is time that you earn, invest and deposit. Credit all which you had been busy debiting and see the rich dividends you earn.

   Don't believe me then try it!

2. **Take Up Challenges:** Knowingly or unknowingly the perfectionism within you has made you a coward of sorts – you have become afraid of taking risks and challenges in your life.

You always fear failure and thus strive to give it your best shot at whatever you are doing but then either you do not succeed in finishing that task or end up unsatisfied with its output. What is life without the risk taking attitude and challenges? You must overcome your fear which in turn will help you in personal development and growth. Do not evaluate performance, just focus on the delights of the activity itself. No one is likely to judge you and they may even like you more if you mess up at times and show your human side! To do away with fear you need to feel the fear and then experience the joy of conquering it. This is the only way to win. So henceforth don't procrastinate in welcoming new challenges – the first challenge being overcoming your perfectionist behaviour.

3. **Enjoy Your Life:** Over the years have you become very serious? Have you diverted all your energies on achieving only? It is good to be serious about your work and also to have a high achievement motivation but it is bad when that is all that is left in your life. You miss out on the small joys and fun life's simple moments has to offer – an evening with old friends, a family get-together, pursuing your hobby or just spending leisure time with your very near and dear ones. It is time now to lighten up and relax. You sure deserve to reward yourself for the hard work you do. Your achievements will be greater and much more if small enjoyments of life are added on to them. Make your relationship with life perfect and not let perfectionism make your life.
4. **Laughter is The Best Medicine:** If you are a perfectionist it is not surprising that you are taking everything in life very seriously. Just recall when you laughed aloud the last time. Smiled to yourself and shared with friends some stupidity you did. Stand in front of the mirror and examine your face. Look for imperfect features and make a funny face at yourself. If an image of yours cannot be perfect how you can expect yourself

to be perfect? Laugh and laugh more at your funny self – 'one who has the ability to laugh at himself is the most perfect of all'. He is perfect in the sense that he is accepting with immense grace the reality of things. You need to wake up to this reality. Laugh and the world will laugh with you but try being perfect and others will laugh at you.

5. **Perfection is Impossible:** If you are a perfectionist then you are imperfectly wasting perfect time over perfecting the art of perfect perfectionism. A perfectionist can never be perfect because perfect perfectionism is imperfectly perfect to the mind of the perfectionist! Confused by this jugglery of words – this is what perfectionism is all about. So get out of this confused state of your being and learn to do things the moderate way – I assure you that you will start performing much better and sooner as well.

In concluding thus chapter all I would like to say is that I have also been a perfectionist. I liked to see order and looked for order everywhere. It was very frustrating because I was never satisfied with the way others did things. Hence I began taking upon myself to do everything till at the end I realized it was getting too stressful. The outcome also was never too satisfactory as per my perfectionist standards. Things began to get delayed and lot of works remained pending. It was not too late and I realized that let work be done as it is being done. At least it will be finished. There is always room for improvement. Old technology is replaced by new one because an improvement has been brought about, not in haste but with due thought, time and patience. We cannot be perfect with the word go and neither can we be perfect in all our doings. So let us accept the things we cannot do perfectly, do perfectly what we can and wisdom to know the difference. In the end of it all you will find that you are finally not only doing things but enjoying doing them as well.

❑❑❑

I'm so dumb !
I can't do
anything !

6

The Low-Esteemed Procrastinator

"Nothing builds self-esteem and self-confidence like accomplishment."

Self-esteem is a term used in psychology to reflect a person's overall emotional evaluation of his or her own worth. It is a judgment of oneself as well as an attitude toward the self. Each of us have a strong need to have stability in our lives, to have a firm base, a high level of self respect, and respect from others. This is the need for self-esteem. If these needs are satisfied, then our self-confidence increases, we feel worthy, strong, capable and adequate as well as find ourselves useful and necessary in the world. On the other hand if these needs are thwarted it leads to one feeling inferior, weak and helpless. If one's self-esteem is high he will willingly attend to all his tasks because it is the accomplishment of tasks which is bringing about his high self esteem and maintaining it as well. If one begins to fail to accomplish tasks, his self-esteem scales down and he loses confidence. This makes him shy away from attending to further tasks.

Let us first test the level of your self-esteem and thereafter relate it with procrastination.

Assess Your Esteem Level

The test below is designed by me to approximately measure your level of self-esteem. Respond to each of the given statement with full truthfulness.

1. Most of the time I am mentally happy. Yes/No.
2. I seldom have health problems such as ulcers. Yes/No.

3. I sleep well during the nights. Yes/No.
4. I do not generally succumb to group pressure for the sake of conformity. Yes/No.
5. I can handle difficult situations without the use of stimulants. Yes/No.
6. I do not consume barbiturates. Yes/No.
7. I take up difficult tasks and see them successfully through. Yes/No.
8. I have a happy go lucky attitude. Yes/No.
9. I don't have many good things to say about myself. Yes/No.
10. Most of the time some problem or the other is bothering me. Yes/No.
11. I suffer from pangs of depression. Yes/No.
12. I have a high level of anxiety. Yes/No.
13. I easily go along with group decisions even if I don't agree with them. Yes/No.
14. At times I feel very insecure. Yes/No.
15. I indulge in self-persecution. Yes/No.
16. I feel most people don't like me. Yes/No.

Scoring and Interpretation

After you have marked your responses give a score of 1 each to the Yes ticked from Qs. 1-8. A score of 1 each to the No ticked from Qs. 9-16. There after total both. If you have scored between 0-4 you have a very low self-esteem. If your score is between 5-10 you are average on self-esteem and if your score is between 11-16 you have a high self-esteem.

Relationship Between Procrastination And Low Self-Esteem

Research has shown that procrastination and self-esteem are

significantly correlated. Low self-esteem seems significantly linked to procrastination. People suffering from feelings of inferiority believe that their failure to perform to stipulated or certain standards, suggest inadequacy to them. To defend self-esteem, they may resort to self-handicap by procrastinating in order to give themselves an external reason, an "out", if they fail.

Examining the components causing procrastination minutely we find that the most common of them reflect the inability to finish tasks, meet deadlines, arrive on time, and keep promises. Poor concentration, negative internal messages, unrealistic expectations, and the inability to organize and work constructively, are present with procrastination. All these are part of an inner system which in turn has many parts to it, self-esteem being an important one. It is not wrong to conclude that procrastination is principally caused by low self esteem and self criticism. Having a low self-esteem makes a person shy away from work because he lacks confidence to believe that he will accomplish the task. However, the dropping of the level of one's self-esteem does not happen overnight. It is important for you to know what causes low-self esteem in order to take corrective measures, if it is bothering you and leading you to procrastinate your work.

Causes of Low Self-esteem

Low self-esteem is caused by certain factors depending on the background and status of the person, his surroundings, age, environment, association with the outside world and varied experiences in childhood and early adolescence. Childhood experiences and a child's upbringing influences self-esteem greatly. An individual with low self-esteem, as a child, believes that important adults and peers in his life have constantly judged him on his performances and successes. He generally felt unloved and valued only when he pleased his parents. Although all children have a need and desire for positive self- esteem, they feel encouraged by the approval they receive from others. They show frustration and feel unloved as a result of other's disapproval. Low self-esteem also creeps in when parents offer acceptance only when a child completes a task or meets a standard; the child feels worthwhile only when the standard is met. Because these standards are conditional, a child's opinion of self is not positively reassured and may then fear attempting new tasks in future. This psychological effect grows on even with adulthood, so does procrastinating behaviour, as an overt indication of low self-esteem– failing to attempt doing tasks!

The bottom line is the negative view of the self that lies at the heart of low self-esteem. Sometimes negative belief about oneself is caused by experiences later on in life, such as workplace bullying or intimidation, abusive relationships, persistent stress or hardship, or traumatic events.

How Low-Self Esteem Causes Procrastination

Individuals suffering from a low self-esteem constantly engage in trying to impress others by seeking their approval in everything they do. However, when such individuals are given negative feedback they begin to believe these negative evaluations as indicators of their ability and self-worth. This in turn becomes direct reflections of their belief that they are incapable, unsuccessful, and unworthy. The two most common responses of such low self-esteem individuals are, firstly, to draw into a shell, feel incompetent and worthless and secondly, feel angry with a desire to get even.

Individuals who feel low generally feel incapable and overwhelmed by the tasks of life so procrastination sets in. Such individuals are shy, prefer to remain where they feel safe, and try to find ways of escaping unpleasant realities or situations, thus shirk responsibilities. Angry responses to low self-esteem include constantly finding fault with the world, be negative about everything, and grudge others. All this combined ultimately amounts to avoidance of task oriented behaviour – procrastination.

Enhancing Self-Esteem Diminishing Procrastination

The reason why procrastination damages your self-esteem, is the fact that although you understand that you need to act today, that there are things that you need to do but for some reason you remain undecided. You may feel safer by not taking action but ultimately you hurt your self-esteem.

A reduction in the esteem level can also lead to procrastination. Such individuals out of frustration accomplish little. To take control over such a situation one needs to identify those factors which are negatively affecting the level of self-esteem. The feelings of fear, rejection, and worthlessness negatively influence the quantum of your self-esteem. If you have found your level of self-esteem to be low and at the same time you tend to be indulging in procrastination it is important that you take steps to enhance your esteem level and thereby diminish procrastination.

Below I am outlining a few ways in which you can enhance your level of self-esteem. You can device your very own mechanisms as well. But what is important is that the level rises constantly and is restored completely.

1. ***Make a list of things you would like to accomplish:*** This is a common method applicable for overcoming most of the reasons which lead to procrastinating behaviour. In this case it is an esteem enhancing one. So get your paper, pen or pencil and begin making a list of all the things you wish to accomplish – I had made mine also before I began writing this book and it led to the completion of this book! After you have made the list prioritize it and then begin to accomplish your mission. When you make your list, be sure to include the consequences you can suffer by procrastinating. Reward yourself when each time you strike off the accomplished things from that list. Seeing the list shorten will do wonders to your esteem – you have succeeded to accomplish what so far you were dreading to begin. However,

this step of enhancement cannot be worked out all by itself. You need to combine it with a few other steps with the right combination – so let us set that combination for you.

2. ***Keep the rewards in mind:*** Once you have drawn out the list of what you wish to accomplish and have prioritized them then the next step is to list the rewards associated with the accomplishments of these tasks. Anticipating what you will benefit upon accomplishing the task will encourage you to exercise your skills towards its accomplishment. Seeing the goal and visualizing the reward will create within you the much wanted desire to work towards attaining it – it will not only act as a catalyst in enhancing your esteem level but also alongside drive your procrastination away.
3. ***Overcome your irrational fears:*** This is a very crucial stage in the enhancement of your self-esteem. Most of the reasons for low self-esteem level relate with imagined and irrational fears and phobias. These irrational fears and phobias give rise to guilt, stress, anxiety and also lead to a drop in the motivational level. These irrational fears and phobias make you lose your self-confidence and compel you to withdraw from taking any action towards accomplishment of your goals. To overcome such fears and phobias you need to first list them out. Further, test them against factual reality and prove to yourself that they are a fragment of your imagination. You need to have courage to take a cold water bath in mild winters but once you begin bathing you don't feel cold for a very long time through the day. You soon become conditioned with the cold water and happily daily take bath with it. So test your fears against reality and you will realize that most of them are unreal. Overcome them and it will help you overcome procrastination.

4. ***Break the cycle of self doubt:*** People who suffer from low self-esteem are constantly being restrained by doubt about their ability. Thoughts like I cannot do it, I will get embarrassed, I will make a fool of myself; I don't have the capability etc. keep popping up now and then. Such pop ups keep damaging the self-esteem. If these thoughts keep popping along and are not controlled then very soon they become delusionary – making one believe in what is actually not a reality. One needs to break this cycle of such negative thoughts and realize what is true. Think differently about yourself and your capabilities. To achieve this focus on all the positives you can gather about yourself and remain focused on them. Ask friends and family to highlight all the positive things that they see in you. Along with charging yourself with positivity you also need to be realistic. You need to be realistic about what might happen after you do attempt to do a task – weigh all pros and cons of your action. This reality testing will help you not get carried away because of over confidence. Make self affirmation your daily exercise and celebrate with each achievement. You will soon see that your self-doubt has turned into self-confidence. Procrastinate doubting yourself. Not your work.
5. ***Indulge in self introspection:*** Look within your own self. Find out what you lack and focus on strengthening your weaknesses. You will find that when you make an effort to overcome your weaknesses you will have more energy and your self-esteem will soar. Procrastination will no longer control your life and you will be motivated to accomplish your goals. You can change your self-image and become a highly motivated individual so take the time to find out why you lack motivation and take steps to improve your self-esteem.

6. ***Spend time with loved ones:*** Spending time with people who value you and really care for you will automatically boost the level of your esteem – it's only after the needs of love, belonging and affection are satisfied can we think and satisfy the need for self-esteem. So basic needs must be fulfilled first.
7. ***Ignore those who scorn you:*** It is very important that we ignore and disregard people who look down upon us. Actually such people themselves suffer from a complex so they envy us. They use scorn as a technique to defeat us – to break us down mentally. So beware! Do not let their scorn bother you and they will be caught in their own web of defeat and dejection. Infect them with the virus of procrastination.
8. ***Always indulge in activities which you find pleasurable:*** Indulging in activities which you find pleasurable brings inner peace and contentment. It relaxes you and rejuvenates the energies to give you a new lease of freshness. Once you are energized you feel better from within and confident as well. This feeling of wellness and confidence is what you need. So do not procrastinate indulging in activities which bring you pleasure.
9. ***Don't depend on others decisions, make your own decisions:*** It is good to seek advice but better to take, make and act upon your own judgment. Taking, making and deciding for yourself will enhance the confidence within you – you will become independent of others and exercise your own reasoning ability and potentials since major part of one's decision taking is influenced by them. When the decision is yours you will act accordingly to live up to the reasons that decision was taken for – No regrets, it is all action. So think like a man of action and defeat procrastinating behaviour.

10. ***Always be true to yourself:*** It is truth that sets you free. If one is not truthful to self and to others he gets captivated within his very own deceptive web. Honesty about self and honesty to self is very essential for one's self-esteem. A distorted picture – negative or positive, never brings about fruitful results. You ultimately deceive only yourself. Face the truth, accept the reality and look forward to ways and means to confront a situation instead of evading it. Evasive attitude will only double your fear and anxiety, and hurt your confidence. So go ahead, wage your war and don't think about winning or losing. Just give it your best shot.

It's a very old saying that everything that happens, it happens for good. It does not mean that bad things happen for good but it means that happenings which even though are not conducive, can be changed into favourable ones if we look at it in a positive manner – the way one looks at situations and himself determines their progress in life. Learn and correct your moves and turn the situation in your favour. Nothing can stop the man with the right mental attitude from achieving his goal; nothing on earth can help the man with the wrong mental attitude. One should not shy away or run away out of fear, worry or due to bad past experiences and failures. All these are teachers and the knowledge one gains through them should be used not to lose but to win and regain the level of self-esteem. He who wins in the end, is one who fought against all odds. A true winner is one who wins over difficult situations and circumstances – so be a true winner and procrastinate defeat and dejection and bring about an enhancement of your worthy self.

❑❑❑

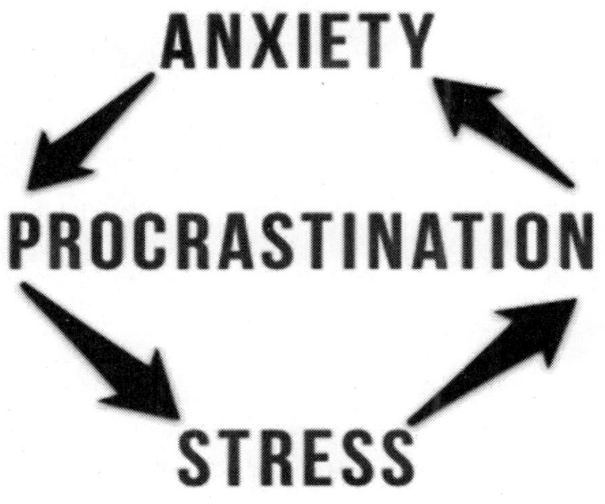
ANXIETY
PROCRASTINATION
STRESS

7

The Anxious Procrastinator

"Putting off an unpleasant task until tomorrow simply gives you more time for your imagination to make a mountain out of a possible molehill. More time for anxiety to sap your self-confidence".

So far, in this book, you have come across many such factors which lead one to procrastinate. However, this chapter will make you look at the factors leading to procrastination in a different manner. It is not that the factors discussed so far and the ones to be discussed ahead are not responsible for procrastination but it is the analysis of procrastination which keeps changing from factor to factor. **Ultimately, the only cause leading to procrastination is the individual's attitude itself which needs to be changed, again by the individual himself.**

Viewing procrastination's relationship with anxiety, we can define it as a silent disease that creeps up with great resilience. It is important to first understand what anxiety is and how it affects our functioning. It is also essential that you measure your anxiety level which will help you understand this concept better and with practical depth. So first measure your level of anxiety.

Measure Your Level of Anxiety

The following test will reveal your present level of anxiety. The statements are based on symptoms, which people suffering from anxiety, display. Being honest in your responses will help you greatly. Remember that this is only a rough measure of your anxiety and not a medical test.

Read each statement carefully and then assign the "point" (0-3) in the blank space provided at the end of each statement. *The point you choose to assign is to be based on the frequency of occurrences with regards to the statement.*

Points

0 – Never.

1 – Sometimes.

2 – Most of the time.

3 – Always.

1. I have difficulty to concentrate on anything. ☐
2. I have difficulty in making decisions. ☐
3. I cannot sleep well during the night. ☐
4. I sweat a lot. ☐
5. My muscles remain in a tensed state. ☐
6. I remain in a state of tension. ☐
7. I worry a lot. ☐
8. I feel uneasy. ☐
9. I am sensitive in interpersonal relationships. ☐
10. I feel inadequate. ☐
11. I feel depressed. ☐
12. I do not take decisions fearing I may make a mistake. ☐
13. My postural movements are strained. ☐
14. I over react to sudden or unexpected things. ☐
15. I shake my legs when sitting. ☐
16. I feel tension in my muscular regions. ☐
17. I profusely perspire in the palms. ☐
18. My blood pressure is high. ☐
19. I suffer from heart palpitations. ☐
20. After taking any decision, I wonder about its appropriateness. ☐

21. I review my mistakes. ☐
22. The past, present and future keeps worrying me. ☐
23. I have nightmares. ☐
24. I have feelings of imminent death. ☐
25. I get fatigued very soon. ☐
26. I keep moving around in the house aimlessly. ☐
27. I am bothered by negative thoughts. ☐
28. My outlook is pessimistic. ☐
29. Small sounds startle me. ☐
30. I suffer from stomach upsets. ☐

Total Score: ☐

Scoring and Interpretation

After you have assigned points to each statement total them up. The following will be your score on this measure. If you have scored in the range of 68 – 90, you are suffering from extreme high anxiety. If you have scored in the range of 46 – 67, you have a high average anxiety. If you have scored in the range of 23 – 45, you have a normal average anxiety level. If you have scored in the range of 0 – 22, then you have low anxiety. Remember this is only an indicator to help you find out if you suffer from anxiety and not a medical/clinical diagnosis.

How Does Anxiety Arise

Anxiety reactions reflect individual's acute feelings of inadequacy in the face of inner and outer stress perceived as threatening. Such reactions are considered normal when the stress situation is sufficiently severe to justify them. Anxiety becomes neurotic and can be considered pathological when it is elicited by stress situations that an average individual handles without much difficulty. Some researches suggest that family history also play a part in increasing the person's chances to develop high levels of anxiety. Trauma and stressful events, such as abuse, the death of a loved one, divorce, changing jobs or schools, may also lead to anxiety.

How Anxiety Leads To Procrastination

You will be surprised to know that anxiety is both, a boon as well as a disorder. What decides its significance is its level. It is a boon when present in average measure, a disorder when it is high and disadvantageous when low or absent. For any individual to function normally and achieve his goals, one has to be anxious about attaining them. It is this anxiety, which provides the driving force. If anxiety is at a normal level then the force exerted by it is beneficial but if the level of anxiety is high it hampers normal functioning leading to behavioural problems and procrastination is one of them. If anxiety is very low or absent there will be no driving force. The individual will not work towards the attainment of his goals and keep on procrastinating.

Procrastination anxiety is the term given to a high anxiety condition that causes the sufferer to 'put off' (defer) an action or event in order to control their high anxiety levels. Procrastination anxiety is actually a misleading name for this condition; it suggests that procrastination causes the anxiety, which is false... in fact, the opposite is true. An underlying high anxiety level causes the flight or fight mechanism to activate 'self-preservation mode' and it is this that causes procrastination anxiety.

The perceptions of individuals exhibiting anxiety symptoms are negatively altered and they thus perceive many things in a negative manner. They expect disaster to occur and worry even over trivial matters. Their outlook becomes pessimistic and they find it impossible to constructively pursue personal or professional work. The worry of such individuals is more than often, unrealistic or out of proportion for the situation. For such individuals life becomes a constant state of worry, fear, and dread. Eventually anxiety dominates their thought process. It interferes with many goals set for their careers, project deadlines, and confidence. In due course of time, it causes them to become chronic procrastinators.

In the context of procrastination, anxiety arises when an individual begins to think about accomplishing a task at hand. No sooner does he begin thinking of doing it he begins to exhibit symptoms of anxiety which makes him feel very uncomfortable. It is not necessary that the individual is even aware that a specific task is triggering this reaction. To bring himself back to a state of equilibrium the individual starts evading that specific task and opts for things which are relaxing for him – watch a television program or even go to sleep.

The reasons for this rise in anxiety level can vary from individual to individual and range from fear of failure, fear of rejection, fear of not attaining perfection, or a fear of leaving his comfort zone. These problems you have already read about earlier but here as related with anxiety, the individual in most cases is not aware as to what exactly is making him anxious. He seeks a solution to get temporary relief from such anxious feeling. This relief comes from postponement of that important task. The mind deceives the individual to feel better by procrastinating. This process becomes a cyclic one because the task in question needs to be done so once again when confronted with doing it the individual becomes anxious and resorts to seeking temporary relief by postponing it. Soon this cyclic process also needs to end ultimately for some very important tasks that crop up. The same feelings repeat but this time the task is done in a hurried manner with disastrous results.

Breaking The Anxiety Based Cycle

It has been said that our anxiety does not empty tomorrow of its sorrow, but only empties today of its strength. Ultimately, does anxiety make one achieve anything at all by procrastinating? One sees himself as a loser when he cannot accomplish anything properly. What he unconsciously feared now became a reality. That reality reinforces this belief in him and his self-confidence drops to the lowest ebb. Reputation gets destroyed and so is trust lost along with credibility. Why take all this pain and wait so long if results are going to be negative. Get going, accomplish the task at hand and I assure you results will be much better and will do good to your self-confidence. Follow the simple advice given and see how you drive the devil of anxiety away and stop procrastinating your work out of baseless fear or worry.

1. ***Restore Confidence in Yourself:*** Many a times anxiety surfaces when you have lost faith in your competence. You begin to worry at each step and stage of the task you are involved with. Develop a positive outlook towards the task which is making you anxious, plan and then execute it systematically. Time spend in this constructive process will enable you to restore your self-confidence and drive your anxiety away.
2. ***Get a Hold on Yourself:*** You know that when confronted with stress arousing situations your nervousness gets the better of you. It is time that you should know one fact - stressful situations make even the strongest of individuals nervous. The secret of success lies in the ability to overcome this anxious state and gracefully perform the task. Hold yourself together and face tough situations with composure.
3. ***Locate the Source of Your Anxiety:*** Many people suffering from generalized anxiety disorder find it hard to locate or identify the anxiety-arousing stimulus. In many cases, the stimulus is not present in fact but is imaginary. In some cases, people develop a fear of facing it when identified. Hence resort to avoidance behaviour. Some, on the other hand do not try identifying the source fearing what it could possibly be. Such type of escapism

or evasive behaviour in fact acts as a catalyst enhancing the levels of anxiety. The best way to tackle anxiety situations is to be honest with yourself, search for the underlying causes, and confront them with confidence. This exercise will also educate you about the reality of the anxiety-arousing situation – whether it is real or imaginary.

4. ***Take Action:*** Normal levels of anxiety compel-us to take action to solve the problem. This action on our part diffuses the anxiety. Even when anxiety levels are high, effort must be made to sooth yourself. A problem exists because a solution for the same is there. Without a solution, a problem has no existence of its own. It is when things get complicated that they turn into problems. Try different methods and approaches to solve your problems. Flexibility is the master key to solutions. Do not give up on problem solving tasks. You surely will succeed. However, many a times when you are confronted with serious problematic situations simple action on your part may fail to solve the same. To successfully handle such situations you have to make use of past experiences and if possible seek help from others. What is ultimately important is that the anxiety-arousing situation should be dealt with and remedied. Problems Pass Away With Time: Nothing is ever permanent because time always moves on. Your problems today will either be resolved or will become outdated. There will be new things to focus your attention on and newer problems also to solve. All you need is the serenity to accept the things you cannot change, courage to change the things you can and above all wisdom to know the difference.

5. ***Yoga, Aerobics, or Simple Exercises Can Help:*** Relaxation therapy though is an important tool of the clinical psychologist, you can also learn to relax on your own. Learn yoga or aerobics and find time to do the same. Yogic exercises will not only relax

your muscles but voluntary meditation will calm your mind. Aerobics and simple exercises keep your physical body in shape. Thus, your physiological and psychological components get relieved of stress and you are energized to tackle and deal efficiently with stressful situations.

If you seriously want to procrastinate procrastination you must strengthen your will and break the anxiety-procrastination cycle or else it will break you mentally. There are little benefits in temporary relief's whereas rewards are positive with outputs. You will have to convince yourself that the tasks at hand are not as hard or difficult as they appear – the difficulty is only an illusion and not real.. This difficult illusion needs to be altered into factual perception which, only awareness of reality can bring about. All you need to do is ignore the negative notions which make you uncomfortable and simultaneously also affirm to yourself that you have the potential and confidence to undertake and accomplish the task. Once you begin the task you yourself will realize that your fears and worries were irrational – a fragment of your imagination. Once this realization comes don't forget to take a hearty laugh at your wild imaginations. In fact laugh your anxiety away.

❑❑❑

DEPRESSION

8

The Depressed Procrastinator

"You can't get much done in life if you only work on the days when you feel good."

Procrastination is related with depression and other maladaptive behaviours. It is a risk factor for depression and perhaps other maladaptive behaviours. However, it still remains to be established whether procrastination is a risk factor or symptom of these syndromes. It is hard to determine this since most studies have been correlated and hence causality cannot be determined. Whatever be it, the fact is that there is a definite link between procrastination and depression. Procrastination may in fact be the beginning of a more serious disorder and can augment symptoms in vulnerable individuals. Often these individuals put off treatment or have severe relapses.

The other side of this complicated picture has some good news as well as bad. One does not necessarily become depressed because he procrastinates. However, if one indulges in excessive procrastination he may, in due course of time, begin to suffer from depression. There is also a high possibility that under depression he is indulging in procrastination. Whatever is the complication in the relationship between procrastination and depression one thing is sure that both lead to delayed action.

Leaving aside the relationship complication for now let me first help you find out if you are depressed or not. If your procrastination score's are on the higher side then this evaluation will in itself help you relate procrastination and depression. The relationship between procrastination and depression will also be discussed in depth further on in this chapter.

Measure Your Depression Level

This is a measure to assess your level of depression. Read each statement carefully and then assign the "point" (0-3) in the blank space provided at the end of each statement. *The point you choose to assign is to be based on the frequency with which you display the characteristic traits in the statement.* Kindly note that this measure has been taken from my book, "Taming The Little Devils Within".

Ratings

0 – Never.

1 – Sometimes.

2 – Most of the time.

3 – Always.

1. I remain sad. ☐
2. Things which were appealing in the past now seem to disinterest me. ☐
3. I don't feel like socializing with my friends. ☐
4. I have a feeling that all good things in my life have ended. ☐
5. I tend to forget even simple things. ☐
6. I am besieged by the fear of my own death. ☐
7. I experience physical discomfort. ☐
8. I feel that I will be unable to perform those tasks which I had performed with perfection in the past. ☐
9. I am overwhelmed by the feeling that I am useless. ☐
10. I am unable to concentrate on anything I do. ☐

11. I get irritated very easily. ☐
12. I have panic attacks. ☐
13. I am burdened by feelings of guilt. ☐
14. I am obsessed by the thought of committing suicide. ☐
15. I have difficulty in going to sleep. ☐

Scoring and Interpretation

After you have assigned the points total them up. This is your score on this measure.

If you have scored in the range of **34 – 45** you are *highly depressed.* If your score is in the range of **23 – 33** you are *moderately depressed.* If it lies in the range of **11 – 22** you are *mildly depressed* and in the range of **0 – 10** you do not seem to suffer from depression at this point of time. Remember this is only an indicator to help you find out if you are depressed. If you have scored high or moderately it is time that you start treatment and talk with your psychiatrist/clinical psychologist.

Note: *The outcome of this test is dependent upon your present set of circumstances and the results obtained need not be generalized for the future. You may be depressed at this point of time but if you handle the situation well you may come out of your depressive mood. Another very important thing is that there are numerous other reasons why one can become depressed and if in case you have obtained a high score on this measure it is not necessary that only procrastination is the cause for the same – it can be just one of the reasons amongst many others.*

How Procrastination Leads To Depression

While responding to the above exercise, you must have noticed that there were many statements in the measure which were also there in the various other tests which you had so far administered on your own in this book. This very fact explains the relationship between procrastination and depression – commonality of symptoms.

Now to explain this relationship further let me put it before you logically. Everyone knows that procrastination is not a positive trait. Once an individual gets into the habit of procrastinating it is quite difficult to break it. Procrastinators end up piling work which in due course of time, leads to more work. They have to rush through to finish the work but rarely enjoy it– in fact they detest doing it. Ultimately out of the pile whichever work is done it is not done properly. It makes their job a very unpleasant one – good riddance to bad rubbish. Procrastinators thus never experience job satisfaction which comes from something done well. The ultimate result is that their level of confidence reduces, they see no reason to celebrate and be happy, things stop appealing to them, and they get overwhelmed by the feeling that they are useless….and have many characteristic traits which are given above in the measure of depression. All in all they begin to feel depressed.

When work is not executed or is delayed it begins to create unnecessary stress, gives rise to anxiety, frustration and procrastination worsens. This in due course of time becomes a cyclical condition, giving rise to the phenomenon known as *depression procrastination*. This state arises when an individual's mind almost totally becomes paralyzed, rendering the individual incapable of performing any work at all. With the onset of depression procrastination the relationship between procrastination and depression becomes inverse – *depression becomes the reason for procrastination.*

How Depression Leads To Procrastination

Depression Procrastination is very much unlike normal procrastination. Like normal procrastination it does not link with any type of fear of failure or fear of success. One can help an individual suffering from normal procrastination by the process of changing their behavioural patterns. This as compared with the problem arising on account of depression is an easy technique. Hence, it can be stated that the problem is diametrically opposite in relation to normal procrastination.

Depression, as mentioned above, compels an individual to experience hopelessness and weariness. Trivial matters ignite his anger and he loses his temper easily. The intention of such individuals then becomes one of giving up everything which they need to do – they isolate themselves from every activity. What is of worry in such a case is that this problem can take a permanent nature with little hope to rectify.

There are many symptoms of depression which feed procrastination. I have already discussed about decision-making. Individuals suffering for depression are numb to feelings of pleasure; they feel that options available to them are all hopeless. This hopelessness in turn can immobilize them – they find starting anything pointless and impossible.

Depression makes procrastination much worse. When he realizes that he is procrastinating and not taking action he feels worse. His depression deteriorates. Because procrastination becomes a mindset, no matter how maladaptive, coping with the emotions and physical symptoms accompanies depression. It may bring some temporary relief, but he eventually wakes up the following day and finds that no fairies have dropped in overnight and done work for him.

Get Going Even When You Are Depressed

It is quite simple to solve the problem of normal procrastination (which we will discuss at length in the last chapter) but solving that of depression procrastination is a very tedious process. It requires very strict measures. The serious aspect of depression procrastination is that it can become of a permanent nature. Depression procrastination cannot be defeated just by changing the behavioural patterns of the concerned person. Overcoming depression procrastination requires a lot of energy, time; effort, pursuance as positive outcome is very slow.

When an individual is depressed, his self-esteem is very low so he begins to doubt his ability to succeed and is more likely to indulge in procrastination.

The tips given below will help individuals to adjust even when they are depressed.

1. ***Reassess your capabilities:*** At times when you are attempting specific work you fail to achieve desired results. This, for many becomes a big setback and shakes their confidence level affecting the outcome of future tasks. The losing of self-confidence then gradually could lead to feelings of depression if it is not boosted. It is best that this problem be nipped in the bud itself. If you have failed once it does not mean you will fail again and again. It is time that you do an honest reassessment of your abilities. This reassessment will surely do good to boost your confidence. It is so important to keep in mind that self-confidence is just a feeling – success enhances it and failures diminish it. So don't resort to procrastinating things to evade failure – go all out and achieve with a firm belief that you can do it.

2. ***Distribute your work:*** Logical management of work is very essential even under normal circumstances. Time and action need to be planned and monitored. You have to evaluate the amount of time you can or should give to particular works and then act in accordance. Do not try to undertake multiple tasks

all at one time. Decide the priority and then accordingly plan, concentrate and execute. Each accomplished task will give you relief and satisfaction of accomplishment. This satisfaction will boost your confidence for doing the next task. So climb the ladder step by step and you will soon find yourself at the top– where you may have doubted to reach but feel happy being there.

3. ***Make yourself ready:*** Mental and physical preparation is a must for indulging in any activity and enjoying it as well. Getting to do work also requires readiness. You will have to turn your mind set towards the task you wish to do. Physically you may need to be energetic so eliminate any trace of fatigue. This mental and physical preparation will create within you a desire to do the required work. Remember when an athlete is going to run in a race, at the starting line it is signalled – ready, get set, go. In the same manner you have to launch yourself on the work track.
4. ***Take breaks:*** When you begin work don't rush at it at one go unless and until it is really urgent. Though it is said that slow and steady wins the race, in your case you may also need to take rest like the rabbit. Begin your work and as it comes on track if you do feel bored then take a short break. Sit back, relax, listen to music or check on what you have done so far. Evaluating your work from time to time will not only provide you some feedback but will also reinforce your concentration. This small break will help you plan your next move as well. Remember that the break should not be too long or you may lose interest in the work you are doing.
5. *Keep a record:* As you progress with your work/s it is very rewarding if you keep a record of all that you have managed.

This record will be proof for you that you have actually done something. Generally when one is depressed he has the feeling that he has not accomplished anything – this record will prove to you that you have indeed accomplished many things, be they big or small.

6. *Celebrate:* Once you have accomplished a task make it a point to celebrate. Do not be disappointed if the task has not been done to perfection but be happy that it has been done. Celebration will not only cheer you but others will also know that you have achieved the goal you had set for yourself – mission accomplished.

Once you get back on the track of doing work, you yourself will be increasing your confidence level. This increase in your confidence level will also do well in driving away your depression. However, if you are depressed, my sincere advice is to find a good psychologist/ psychiatrist and get treatment at the earliest. With the cure of your depression procrastination will also vanish.

❑❑❑

NEXT WEEK
TOMORROW
OTHER DAY
NOW
SOMEDAY
IN THE FUTURE
NEXT YEAR
LATER

9

The Indecisive Procrastinator

"Nothing is as exhausting as indecision, and nothing so futile. When you have to make a choice and don't make it, that in itself is a choice creating a conflict."

Procrastination almost always reveals an inner conflict about whatever it is you are putting off. Part of you wants to get the job done, while another part is hesitating. As mentioned before and as is being repeated line by line here, is that, decisive procrastinators engage themselves wholeheartedly in searching for more information about various topical alternatives before they come to any final decision and that is, if they do make one at all. The strategy adopted by decisional procrastinators lead them to a more confused state of the mind and they end up falling prey to self-sabotage. With the many options that they have explored and have at hand, they succumb to what is termed as optional paralysis. They create so many choices for themselves that they feel unable to decide, for fear of choosing an option that is less than perfect. Thus, this optional paralysis paralyses the entire functional machinery leading to no or delayed outputs.

Some Common Inner Conflicts Underlying Procrastination

Inner conflicts which are self generated by a procrastinator may be due to any or a combination of the reasons listed below.

Fear of being criticized: A procrastinator may harbour an unrealistic feeling that once his work is complete it will become vulnerable to criticism by others. As long as he is slowly carrying on with the work he feels secure and so keeps delaying it. Thus, the fear of being criticized at times may give rise to conflicts which enable him to still carry on with his work and safeguard his ego from being hurt.

Fear of being successful: Many people have an unconscious fear that if they achieve success then other people may not take it in the right spirit. The fear of displeasing others holds them back from accomplishing the work at hand. The conflict they undergo is approach-avoidance type in which they do want to accomplish the work but the fear of negative reactions makes them avoid the accomplishment.

Fear of failure: The fear of failure is a very common phenomenon in procrastinators. They fear that even after putting in their best they may fail in achieving the desired results. This fear compels them to look for excuses on a conscious or unconscious level, to evade doing the work.

Belief systems and comfort zones: Many procrastinators keep on reinforcing the belief that they are procrastinators. This reinforced attitude enables them to block themselves from concentrating on any work. If the work does not begin at all they feel safer in their comfort zone – a state of inertia.

Fear of increased expectations: Many individuals irrationally fear that if they succeed in accomplishing a given task they will attract more expectations from others. This increase in expectations will in turn burden them with more assignments which simply are of no interest to them. They evade such a situation, and intentionally procrastinate their work at hand. This creates a negative impression on others.

Measure for Decisional Conflict

What you need to know is how the process of conflict operates on a psychological level if you have to overcome this type of procrastinating behaviour. *Another important point to mention here is that it is not necessary that decisional conflicts arise only with procrastinators – normal and healthy individuals at times succumb to it as well.* To enable you to understand decisional conflicts it is necessary that first you measure yourself on the same. The measure will tell you about your personal perceptions of: uncertainty in choosing options, modifiable factors contributing to uncertainty such as feeling uninformed, unclear about personal values and unsupported in decision making and, finally effective decision making such as sensing the choice is informed, value-based, likely to be implemented and expressing satisfaction with the choice.

The measure for decisional conflict has been developed by O'Connor A.M. and is known as Traditional Decisional Conflict Scale, published as – Validation of a decisional conflict scale. Med. Dec. Making 1995: 15(1): 25-30. The classic psychometric paper. It has the permission for use with the condition that the above reference is cited. However, some statements (items) of the scale have been modified by me for suitability purpose. The scoring and interpretation remain as stated in the original scale.

Below are given statements (items) which may/may not describe you. For each statement, decide whether the statement is characteristic or uncharacteristic of you and then express your agreement/disagreement to the same. Remember to be honest with your response.

1. I am always clear about the options that are available to me. *Strongly Agree/Agree/Neutral/Disagree/Strongly Disagree.*
2. I am clear about the benefits of the options that are available to me. *Strongly Agree/Agree/Neutral/Disagree/Strongly Disagree.*
3. I am clear about the risks and dangers involved with options available. *Strongly Agree/Agree/Neutral/Disagree/Strongly Disagree.*
4. I am clear about which benefits matter most to me. *Strongly Agree/Agree/Neutral/Disagree/Strongly Disagree.*

5. I am clear about which risks and dangers matter most. *Strongly Agree/Agree/Neutral/Disagree/Strongly Disagree.*
6. I am clear about which is more important to me (the benefits or the risks and dangers). *Strongly Agree/Agree/Neutral/Disagree/Strongly Disagree.*
7. I have enough support from others to make a choice. *Strongly Agree/Agree/Neutral/Disagree/Strongly Disagree.*
8. I chose my option without pressure from others. *Strongly Agree/Agree/Neutral/Disagree/Strongly Disagree.*
9. I get enough advice to make a choice. *Strongly Agree/Agree/Neutral/Disagree/Strongly Disagree.*
10. I am clear about the best choice for me. *Strongly Agree/Agree/Neutral/Disagree/Strongly Disagree.*
11. I feel sure about what to choose. *Strongly Agree/Agree/Neutral/Disagree/Strongly Disagree.*
12. I find it easy to make decisions. *Strongly Agree/Agree/Neutral/Disagree/Strongly Disagree.*
13. I feel that I make informed choices. *Strongly Agree/Agree/Neutral/Disagree/Strongly Disagree.*
14. My decisions show what is important for me. *Strongly Agree/Agree/Neutral/Disagree/Strongly Disagree.*
15. I always stick to what I have decided. *Strongly Agree/Agree/Neutral/Disagree/Strongly Disagree.*
16. I am always satisfied with the decisions I make. *Strongly Agree/Agree/Neutral/Disagree/Strongly Disagree.*

Scoring and Interpretation

After you have marked your responses assign points as such: 0 = strongly agree; 1 = agree; 2 = neutral; 3 = disagree; 4 = strongly disagree.

After you have assigned scores for each statement sum them up. This will give your total score. After you have summed up the 16 items **[1-16]** divide (÷) this total by 16. After you have done this multiply (x) it by 25. This formula expresses your obtained score as a percentage. Scores range from **0** (*no decisional conflict*) to **100** (*extremely high decisional conflict*).

To find out your score and interpretation of the sub categories, follow the instructions given very carefully and avoid making any mistake.

***Uncertainty* Sub-score:** Add the scores of item number **10, 11 and 12** then divide (÷) this total by 3. After you have done this multiply (x) it by 25. This formula expresses your obtained score as a percentage. Scores range from **0** (*extremely certain about best choice*) to **100** (*extremely uncertain about best choice*).

***Informed* Sub-score:** Add the scores of item number **1, 2 and 3** then divide (÷) this total by 3. After you have done this multiply (x) it by 25. This formula expresses your obtained score as a percentage. Scores range from **0** (*extremely informed*) to **100** (*extremely uninformed*).

***Values* Clarity Sub-score:** Sum of the scores of item number **4, 5 and 6** then divide (÷) this total by 3. After you have done this multiply (x) it by 25. This formula expresses your obtained score as a percentage. Scores range from **0** (*extremely clear about personal values for benefits and risks*) to **100** (*extremely unclear about personal values for benefits and risks*).

Support *Sub-score:* Add the scores of item number **7, 8 and 9** then divide (÷) this total by 3. After you have done this multiply (x) it by 25. This formula expresses your obtained score as a percentage. Scores range from **0** (*extremely supported in decision making*) to **100** (*extremely unsupported in decision making*).

***Effective* Decision Sub-score:** Add the scores of item number **13, 14, 15 and 16** then divide (÷) this total by 4. After you have done this multiply (x) it by 25. This formula expresses your obtained score as a percentage. Scores range from **0** (*good decision*) to **100** (*bad decision*).

THE CONCEPT OF DECISIONAL CONFLICT

You have just evaluated yourself on certainty about choices, being informative about the options available, clear about personal values and risks involved, the support you receive in making decisions and finally your decision making ability. If you have scored on the lower side, say less than 40 then these factors may not be responsible for your procrastinating behaviour. However, if you have scored above 40 then you need to understand the involvement of these factors in your procrastinating behaviour.

WHAT EXACTLY IS DECISIONAL CONFLICT?

Decisional conflicts arise when one is unable to decide upon the course of action. The probability of such an uncertainty increases when a person is confronted with decisions involving risk or uncertainty of outcomes, when high-stakes choices with significant potential gains and losses are entertained, when there is a need to make valuable trade-offs in selecting a course of action, or when anticipated regret over the positive aspects of rejected options is probable.

The main behavioural manifestations of decisional conflict include verbalization of uncertainty about choices, verbalization of the undesired consequences of alternatives, indecisiveness between choices, and delayed decision making. Minor manifestations include verbalized distress while attempting decision making, self-focus, physical signs of distress or tension, and questioning personal values and beliefs while attempting to make a decision.

Procrastinators unintentionally open up many options for working upon a task. These multiple options bring about a dilemma since alternatives may have both desirable and undesirable outcomes. They may also have desirable outcomes occurring partly with one option and partly with another. In such a case no alternative satisfies their personal objective and they fail to come to a conclusive decision. This situation is technically termed as *'choice dilemma'* which is characterized by: the *risks* or uncertainty about benefits or harm; the need to make *value judgments* about potential benefits versus potential harms and finally anticipated *regret* over the positive aspects of rejected options.

The uncertainty becomes intense when the procrastinator feels uninformed about the alternatives, benefits and risks associated with the choices he has happily created. Vagueness about his own personal values also acts as a stumbling stone and finally lack of support from others in making a choice or the pressure to choose the course of action create stress upon him.

Factors Contributing To Decisional Conflict

There are many factors which contribute to *decisional conflict* but mainly it arises from two sources:

1. ***Inherent Difficulty:*** People are uncertain because of the inherent difficulty of the choice with both positive and negative effects. For example, going or not going on a pilgrimage to a far of place located in rough terrain may become a matter of a choice conflict. The positive side may be blessings of the Almighty but the negative aspect of harsh conditions would have to be endured to reach there. Procrastinators or even normal people may have a decisional conflict regarding the pilgrimage leading to psychological distress.

2. ***Modifiable Factors:*** There are several modifiable factors which make an inherent difficult decision even more difficult.

    - *Lack of knowledge:* Even a procrastinator with ample information would suffer lack of knowledge with regards to the potential outcomes of the multiple options he has in hand.

- *Unrealistic expectations:* A procrastinator harbours unrealistic expectations or perceptions of the likelihood of outcomes. He tends to exaggerate or minimize chances of outcomes by either generalizing all or by questioning the probabilities of each.
- *Unclear values:* The procrastinator is unclear about his very own personal values. He is also unclear about the personal importance or the desirability of outcomes.
- *Unclear perceptions of others:* The procrastinator has difficulty in understanding other people. He is unclear about the opinions given by them. He is also unclear as to the mode others would adopt in the same situation to achieve the goal.
- *Social pressure:* Many a times a procrastinator has difficulty in withstanding social pressure for choosing one of the options available. This seems like a forced choice to him. He constantly tries to evade the situation but ultimately chooses an option which he himself is not convinced about.
- *Lack of support:* The procrastinator may sense a lack of support or mismatch between preferred and actual role in decision making. He perhaps feels that his family, friends or colleagues are not being supportive of him to help him resolve his conflicts or take a conclusive decision.
- *Lack of skills and low self-confidence:* The procrastinator many at times create a situation which he feels is novel. He then realizes that he has never handled anything such before and begins to doubt his own abilities in handling it.
- *Lack of other resources:* Many a times a procrastinator finds excuses that resources are lacking for doing or completing the required task at hand.

Overcoming Decisional Conflicts

There is a very old saying in English –"Forty people can take a horse to the well but they cannot make him drink". The horse needs to feel thirsty to drink! The same applies to people who exhibit procrastinating behaviour. In the first place they have themselves paved the way and given rise to conflicts which hamper their decision making ability. It is so important not to create such conflicting situations. Even if conflicting situations do arise due to circumstances they can be well sorted out.

The following points will help not only procrastinators take decisions in a better manner but also non-procrastinators.

1. Whenever there is doubt about how tasks have to be done don't hesitate to seek genuine information about the options available for accomplishing the same.
2. Seek information related with the benefits, risks and side-effects of the option you are going to choose for accomplishing the task.
3. Clear your values. This can be done by describing outcomes in sufficient details to better judge their value. This value judgment includes physical, emotional, and social impacts.
4. Don't feel shy to seek support and directions on how to accomplish your task.
5. Stop creating self conflicts because they are the core cause of procrastinating behaviour.

The next time you are confronted with stressful situations, which require decisions on a daily basis, and you are bombarded with decision making situations consistently, you seek escape by creating conflicts, to delay your decision and action, remember that nothing is as fatiguing as the eternal hanging on of an uncompleted task because every duty which is bidden to wait returns with seven fresh duties at its back. The best way to get something done is to begin it right away because putting off an easy thing makes it hard and putting off a hard thing makes it impossible. You will never have more time. You have, and have always had, all the time there is. No purpose is served in waiting until next week or even until tomorrow. Keep going day in and day out. Concentrate on something useful. Make a decision and having decided to accomplish a task, accomplish it at all costs – costs will keep increasing if you delay. So make the best bargain.

Be Your Own Director!!

10

Procrastination and Self-Regulatory Failure

"The way to get started is to quit talking and begin doing."

To begin this chapter let me first ask a question to those of you who have so far found yourself to be non-procrastinators on the measures you have administered on yourself. The question is very simple and straightforward – "*I never procrastinate.*" True/False. I really wonder how many of you have answered *true* because the ratio is going to be really very low. If you have answered true then you are a rare specimen but at the same time it points a needle of suspicion upon you. You may eiher be lying or responding in a socially desirable fashion. It is very rare to come across any such individual who does not indulge in procrastination because it is a universal human foible and thus becomes an interesting thing related with failure to self-regulate. It is important to first understand deeply the concept of self-regulation in order to understand how its failure leads to procrastination.

What Is Self-Regulation

Self-regulation is the self's capacity for altering its behaviours. It greatly increases the flexibility and adaptability of human behaviour, enabling people to adjust their actions to a remarkably broad range of social and situational demands. It is an important basis for the popular conception of free will and for socially desirable behaviour. It provides benefits to the individual and to society, and indeed good self-control seems to contribute to a great many desirable outcomes, including task performance, academic and work success, popularity, mental health and adjustment, and good interpersonal relationships. Self-regulation failure on the other hand is the absence of all that self-regulation achieves.

MEASURE YOUR SELF-REGULATION

Before I make you aware about self-regulation and how its failure is related with procrastination, it is important for you to measure your very own self-regulation level. The test is a very brief one designed specifically *to measure your self-regulation in relation to procrastination.* Read each statement carefully and assign the appropriate weight based upon its applicability to you. The weights to choose from are given below and to be assigned by you after each statement in the space provided thereafter. Remember that your honesty is also a part of self-regulatory behaviour.

Not at all true – 1

Barely true – 2

Moderately true – 3

Exactly true – 4

1. When required I can focus my attention on one activity for a long time. ☐
2. I am able to accomplish goals I set for myself. ☐
3. In case I get distracted while doing work I can quickly gather my concentration and carry on doing the work without hindrance. ☐
4. When I plan to work, I remove all the things that are not relevant to my work. ☐
5. If an activity arouses my feelings too much, I can calm myself down so that I can continue with the activity soon. ☐

6. It's not difficult for me to wait for my turn in a queue for a long time. ☐
7. If an activity requires a problem-oriented attitude, I can control my feelings. ☐
8. When I have a problem, I think of different ways to take care of the problem. ☐
9. It is not difficult for me to suppress thoughts that interfere with what I need to do. ☐
10. I am able to work effectively toward long-term goals. ☐
11. I can control my thoughts from distracting me from the task at hand. ☐
12. Even if I worry about something, I can concentrate on an activity. ☐
13. After an interruption, I don't have any problem resuming my concentrated style of working. ☐
14. I keep focused on tasks I need to do even if I do not like them. ☐
15. No amount of external disturbances can interfere with my ability to work in a focused way. ☐
16. Even personal problems don't distract me from my plan of action and I stay focused on my goal. ☐

SCORING AND INTERPRETATION

After having assigned the weights add all of them. This will give you your total score on self-regulation. If you have obtained a score between **64-48** you are high on self-regulation, a score between **47-32** you are average and a score between **31-16** you are low on self-regulation which means self-regulation failure in relation to work/ tasks.

THE INGREDIENTS OF SELF-REGULATION

There are basically three ingredients which govern self-regulation along with a flavourful topping of motivation which we will discuss at length separately in the next chapter.

1. ***Standards***: The definition of *self regulation* indicates change to arrive at some standard. In line with this, effective self-regulation requires a clear and well-defined standard. When standards are ambiguous, uncertain, inconsistent, or conflicting they tend to make self-regulation difficult. Another important possibility is that different standards can alter emotional reactions and behavioural processes.
2. ***Monitoring***: Self-regulation requires monitoring because if we do not do so it will become very difficult to regulate behaviour. Thus, it is very important that we maintain behaviour check. How this is done and brought into operation is explained by the *feedback-loop theory of human self-regulation*. A person performs a test by comparing the self (or the relevant aspect of self) to the standard. If the self falls short, then self-regulation requires initiating some exercise to upraise the self in order to match the standard.. Further tests evaluate progress toward meeting the goal, and eventually confirm that the self has reached the standard sought, whereupon no further attempts are required, and so the exercise can cease.
3. ***Willpower***: This is also known as *self-regulatory strength*. The exercise aimed at upraising the self are difficult and therefore require some power. Regulating the self appears to depend on a limited resource that operates like a strength or energy and becomes temporarily depleted afterward, thus creating the state of ego depletion. Recent research has indicated that blood glucose, which is the brain's principal source of fuel, is

an important component of this resource: Acts of self-control consume substantial quantities of glucose, resulting in lower levels of it in the bloodstream.

4. ***Motivation***: Here motivation more specifically means, motivation to achieve the goal or meet the standard, which in practice amounts to *'motivation to regulate the self'*. Even if the standards are clear, monitoring is fully effective, and the person's resources are abundant, he or she may still fail to self-regulate because of inadequate desire to accomplish goal. (*We will discuss about motivation and procrastination at length in the next chapter.*)

For effective self-regulation some of each of the four ingredients is necessary – it is exactly like the spices which are added to make meals, not less and not too much but the right quantity. Unlike spices, it is possible that the four requisites can compensate or substitute for each other to some degree. If motivation is high, such as if the person really and strongly wants to measure up to some standard, this may compensate for a somewhat lower than normal level of willpower or a greater difficulty of monitoring. For example, alcohol impairs self-regulation substantially by impairing the monitoring of one's behaviour and so an intoxicated person may be prone to say or do things undesirable. However, if motivation is strong – then perhaps even if the person's boss or father-in-law unexpectedly enters the scene – the person may still manage to speak carefully and properly, despite difficulty. However, every ingredient is not interchangeable and this interchange also could depend from situation to situation. Motivation may not be enough to substitute for lack of clear standard. That combination would mean someone wanting to self-regulate but not knowing what desirable responses to enact where.

Self-Regulation Failure

By now you must have understood that *self-regulation failure* is the absence of standards, lack of monitoring, willpower and motivation.

These all together are the driving forces of one's behaviour. If they are absent or low then it becomes difficult for an individual to regulate his behaviour. Failure to regulate, probably will also lead to procrastination besides other things. Individuals low on self-regulation find it difficult to make plans, encounter conflict when they have to choose from alternatives, they lack control over their impulses, have difficulty inhibiting unwanted thoughts and fail in regulating their social behaviour. You have come across most of these failures while going through previous chapters and now can relate it in totality with procrastination.

Acquisition of Self-Regulation Skills For Overcoming Procrastination

Self-regulation failure is one of the most likely reasons for procrastinating behaviour because it includes various causes which lead to procrastination. It thus becomes important not only for procrastinators but even non-procrastinators to develop and practice self-regulation skill. This is a phase oriented plan and should be followed in the order of the phase given. One cannot jump right across a phase in a hurry because then the plan will not work. Kindly note, that this plan is focused specifically in developing self-regulation from the standpoint of overcoming procrastination. It does not apply to acquisition of self-regulation skills in its totality.

First Phase – Readiness: In this phase some situations appear where you have to mentally ready yourself to perform the specific task or activity. You need to organize all preparatory adjustments which will immediately precede the action required on your part. These preparations include reflecting on your past experiences, if any, related with that specific work at hand. You need to mentally tune yourself for doing that work and also ensure that the settings in which you have to do the work are well organized. If they are not well organized then do the needful but do not go about being a perfectionist – do whatever you can do with the little you have around you and you will succeed doing much more in the end. Once you are ready on the above counts it will create a desire within you to do that specific task or activity – *it means a mental preparation for action.*

Second Phase – Planning, Organizing and Transforming Information: Once you are mentally prepared to do a task then begin with the work of planning, organizing and transforming information. This phase precedes the actual performance; sets the stage for action; maps out the tasks to minimize the unknown; and also helps to further develop a positive mindset. Realistic expectations can make the task more appealing. Goals must be set as specific outcomes, arranged in order from short-term to long-term. To go about doing this you need to first outline your plan of action, summarize it, rearrange your material and tools if needed accordingly, draw out a sequence plan also including the time required for completion of the task or activity. If the task is very difficult to do or risky always have a backup plan at hand.

Third Phase – Keeping Records and Monitoring: This phase is implemented while the work is progressing. You need to allot time to make notes of things which you have done, left undone or even need to do more than planned. You should evaluate your work for errors if any, so that you can rectify them. You must monitor yourself and focus on it. The time you take should also be monitored and efficiently utilized. Finally, while doing the work you will begin to realize under what conditions you are accomplishing the most – make the best use of that.

Phase Four – Self Evaluation: This phase involves reflection after the performance, a self-evaluation of outcomes compared to goals. Once your work is done you need to evaluate the outcome as against what you had planned out. You need to look at the records and check if you were distracted and how you overcame it. Time management skills also must be evaluated. Did you finish the task in the time frame you allowed yourself? The conditions under which you accomplished the work should be looked into carefully. Finally you need to do your task evaluation in terms of its effective outcome. Evaluate your output and see if it satisfies you. After you have done all this you will gather enough feedback for future reference. It will also motivate you when you see what all you have done and how you have achieved it. If you have erred at places take it positively and as a learning experience – you have learned how to rectify your mistake. What is important is that you accomplished what you had been procrastinating and that in itself is the biggest achievement and reward for you.

This is not all there is to acquisition of self-regulation skills for overcoming procrastination. You need to work upon developing your very own plan which you can use to enhance your self-regulation with. You may have to combine various strategies which best suit you. You also need to look into some common self-regulation strategies that have worked well for other successful people which can help even you to be successful like them. Do an honest self assessment about your strengths and weaknesses. The weaknesses should be acknowledged by you and worked upon. If procrastination is holding you back, identify the factors responsible for that and try bringing about improvisation. Finally I can only guide you but it is you who has to regulate yourself. So take on the driving seat, drive while following the rules and you will reach your destination safely and happily.

❑❑❑

I can... but I won't

11

The Motivated Procrastinator

*"If you have goals and procrastination you have nothing.
If you have goals and you take action,
you will have anything you want."*

A procrastinator's will-power lies in the fact that he keeps work pending because he strongly feels he wants to do the same – keep it pending. When one agrees that he is supposed to perform an activity, understands all about that activity and above all admits there is a need to perform that activity and yet significantly fails to perform that activity within the desired or expected time frame then that amounts to procrastination. Procrastination of this attitude indicates a *motivational problem* of more than just poor time management skills or inherent laziness. Although individuals endorsed many different reasons for procrastinating, the majority of reasons translate as fear of failure. However, other motivational factors besides fear of failure also contribute to the problem of procrastination.

Thirteen Negative Motivation Patterns

Motivation is an important part of one's daily life. Most of us know quite a lot about the positive side and effects of motivation but very few are aware of its negative side. To help overcome procrastination it is much too essential that this negative side of motivation be understood and understood very clearly. Knowing the set of negative motivation patterns will surely help you identify counter-productive self-talk that can get in the way of your taking action in overcoming procrastination.

Dr. David D. Burns in his book *Feeling Good*: *The New Mood Therapy Revised and Updated* has identified 13 procrastination and doz.-nothingism mindsets and also explains each one of them as such:

- *Hopelessness* – Any activity will seem pointless because you are absolutely certain your lack of motivation and sense of oppression are unending and irreversible.
- *Helplessness* – You cannot possibly do anything to make yourself feel better because you are convinced that your moods are caused by factors beyond your control, such as fate, hormone cycles, dietary factors, luck, and other people's evaluations of you.
- *Overwhelming Yourself* – You may magnify a task to such a degree that it could seem impossible to tackle. You may again assume that you must do everything at once instead of breaking each job down into small, discrete, manageable unit which you can complete one step at a time. You might inadvertently distract yourself from the task at hand by obsessing about endless other things you have not managed to do so far. *Jumping to Conclusions* – You sense that it is not within your power to take effective action that will result in satisfaction because you are in the habit of saying, "I cannot" or "I would but …"
- *Self-labelling* – The more you procrastinate, the more you degrade yourself as inferior. The problem is compounded when you label yourself as "a procrastinator" or "a lazy person." This makes you view your lack of effective action as the "*real you*" *so* that you automatically expect little or nothing from yourself.
- *Undervaluing the Rewards* – You feel the reward simply wouldn't be worth the effort.
- *Perfectionism* – You defeat yourself with inappropriate goals and standards.
- *Fear of Failure* – Because you imagine that putting in the effort but not succeeding would be an overwhelming personal

defeat, you refuse to try at all. Several misunderstood notions are responsible for fear of failure. One of the most common is over-generalization. For example, you reason, "If I fail at this, it means I will fail at anything." This of course is impossible. Nobody can fail at everything. A second mind-set that contributes to the fear of defeat is when you evaluate your performance exclusively on the outcome regardless of your individual effort. This is illogical and reflects as "product orientation" rather than a "process orientation".

- *Fear of Success* – Because of your lack of confidence, success may seem even more questionable than failure because you are certain it is based on chance. You may also fear success because you anticipate people will make even greater demands on you. Because you feel convinced that you either have to meet their expectations or may fail to meet their expectations, success could put you into a dangerous and impossible situation. Therefore, you try to maintain control by avoiding any commitment or involvement.
- *Fear of Disapproval or Criticism* – You imagine that if you try something new, any mistake or flub will be met with strong disapproval or criticism because the people you care about won't accept you if you are human and imperfect. The risk of rejection seems so dangerous that to protect yourself you adopt as low a profile as possible. If you don't make any effort, you can't goof up.
- *Coercion and Resentment* – A deadly enemy of motivation is a sense of coercion. You feel under intense pressure to perform – generated from within and without. This happens when you try to motivate yourself with moralistic "should" and "ought." You tell yourself, "I should do this" and "I have to do that." Then you feel obliged, burdened, tense, resentful and guilty. You feel like

a delinquent child under the discipline of a tyrannical probation officer. Every task becomes coloured with such unpleasantness that you cannot face it.

- Then, as you procrastinate, you condemn yourself as a lazy, no-good person. This further drains your energies.
- *Low Frustration Tolerance* – Your frustration results from your habit of not being realistic but imagination of some idealistic feature in your head. When the two don't match, you condemn or disregard reality. It doesn't occur to you that it may be infinitely easier to change your expectations rather than to bend and twist actual facts.
- *Guilt and Self-blame* – If you are frozen in the conviction that you are no good or have let others down, you will naturally feel unmotivated to pursue your daily life.

Motivation To Procrastinate

How can one's motivation influence procrastination? It may sound strange but at times procrastination is the result of a negative motivation – it is a motivation after all. This motivation conditions the individual into not acting. How this influences procrastination has a very simple explanation. One's level of motivation is the result of two competing forces that are constantly changing and interacting with each other inside the mind: the drive or desire to take action and one's resistance to take action, which usually comes from fear, anxiety, overwhelm, doubt and avoidance of potential pain.

If one's drive to take action is stronger than the resistance then he will feel naturally motivated to take the actions he wants. It is a win-win situation – you win.

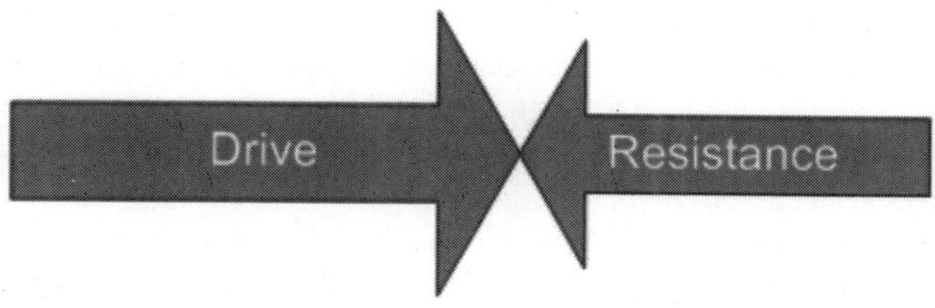

However if one's resistance is stronger than his drive, he most likely will procrastinate or avoid taking action - even if he desperately so desires. Fully knowing that taking action is good for him he will be far better off by not doing it. It is a losing situation – procrastination wins.

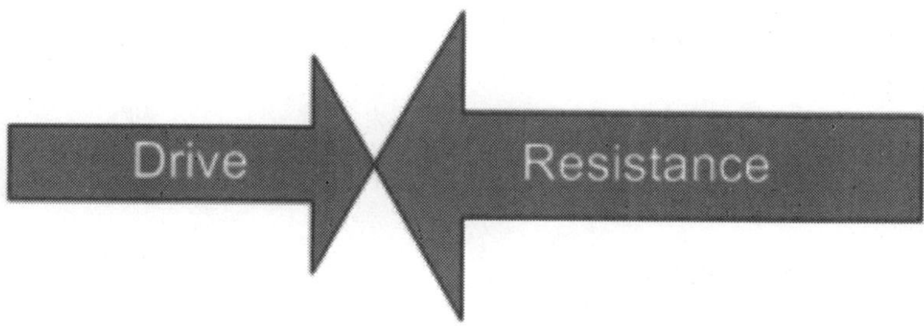

The fact that you want to take action... but you just cannot get yourself to do so is what makes procrastination so difficult and so frustrating.

Most people struggle with procrastination and feel as though they have no conscious control over their own actions beçause they *don't understand the source of their motivation* - they know not what is pushing them in one direction or pulling them in another... and they definitely do not know how to tip the scales in their favour and make it easier to take actions as they want..

The good news is that you already have much more control over these two forces than you may realize... but you need to understand how they work and learn a few simple but very powerful techniques to quickly and easily boost your drive and lower your resistance. In order to be able to understand these forces of motivation, you need to first put yourself through a test.

Test Your Motivated Procrastination

The following test is to help you identify which type of *motivated procrastinator* you are – *selective achievement oriented* or *selective avoidance oriented*. This in turn will help you understand your procrastination related with motivation, much justifiably so as to help you overcome it.

Read each statement carefully and assign the appropriate weight based upon its applicability to yourself. The weights to choose from are given below and to be assigned by you after each statement in the space provided thereafter. Remember that your honesty is very important.

Points

0 – Never.

1 – Sometimes.

2 – Most of the time.

3 – Always.

1. You seek challenges in life. ☐
2. You fight to the finish. ☐
3. You value the feedback others give to you. ☐
4. You enjoy evaluation sessions of your work progress/output. ☐
5. You are not afraid of failure in your works. ☐
6. You take responsibility for all your actions. ☐
7. You believe your performance to be within your control. ☐
8. You believe success is achieved through efforts. ☐

9. You believe that failure is due to lack of concentration. ☐
10. You look at things in a positive manner. ☐
11. You are confident about your abilities. ☐
12. You complete your tasks quickly. ☐
13. You complete your tasks efficiently. ☐
14. You seek to take up only those tasks which are possible to do. ☐
15. You work towards achieving a goal. ☐

Scoring

After you have assigned the points total them up. Read your score as follows. If you have scored in the range of 34 – 45 you have a *high selective achievement orientation**. If your score is in the range of 23 – 33 you have a *moderate selective achievement orientation**. If it lies in the range of 11 – 22 you have a *moderate selective avoidance orientation** and in the range of 0 – 10 you have a *high selective avoidance orientation**.

Remember your scores are only indications of your level and direction of motivation and not actual predictors of the same.

Interpretation

* *High selective achievement orientation* – this means that you do have a high achievement orientation and possess the characteristics of high need achievers but then your task selection is based upon probability of success, an intermediate difficulty level, and the incentive associated with success. You tend to be selectively avoiding or procrastinating those tasks where you think probability of success is low, the task appears too difficult to accomplish and incentives not too lucrative.

* *Moderate selective achievement orientation* –You do have a moderate achievement orientation and possess the characteristics of

moderate need achievers. Your task selection is based upon moderate probability of success, an intermediate difficulty level, and the incentive associated with success. You tend to be selectively avoiding or procrastinating those tasks where you think that probability of success is low, the task appears too difficult to accomplish and incentives not too lucrative.

* *Moderate selective avoidance orientation* – Even though you may be having a moderate achievement orientation you are also inclined more towards avoiding failure. Because of this avoidance for fear of failure, you tend to choose only those tasks which are very simple and in which probability of failure is negligible or on the other hand very difficult tasks, where the humiliation of failure is less. All other tasks are selectively being avoided or being procrastinated.

* *High selective avoidance orientation* – Even though you may be having a high achievement orientation you also are highly inclined to avoid failure. Because of this avoidance for fear of failure, you tend to choose only those tasks which are very simple and in which probability of failure is negligible or on the other hand very difficult tasks, where the humiliation of failure is less. All other tasks are selectively being avoided or being procrastinated.

Motivated Selective Procrastination

Psychologists may agree or disagree with the theory of *motivated selective procrastination* which I have been investigating into, and its fusion with the characteristics which individuals with achievement orientation possess. Logically it is reasonable to suggest that the selective task oriented behaviour of such achievement oriented individuals lead them to intentionally avoid or procrastinate other tasks with which they are not comfortable, or in which probability of success is low. On the other hand those achievement oriented individuals who are high on avoiding failure, also are selective about which task they should perform and which they should avoid or procrastinate. In short, procrastination becomes a selected motivated behaviour even in individuals who are motivated to achieve.

The positive drive one has within him is a sign of his motivation to achieve, and, on the other hand his resistance indicates a fear of failure lurking deep within. This fear brings about an overt tendency of avoidance for any task which though may seem appealing and yet increase his intensity of anxiety, thus creating a negatively motivated state of selective action or inaction.

Ones positivity of action rests upon three things: First, the individual's motive to succeed or need of achievement. Second, his estimate about the likelihood of success in performing a particular task, and lastly, the incentive for success. On the other hand the negativity related with action is the outcome of the tendency to avoid failure. This also rests upon three things: Firstly the individual's motive to avoid failure. Second, his estimate of the likelihood of failure at that particular task and lastly the incentive value of failure at that task – how unpleasant it would be to fail.

Now selective action or inaction will depend upon the relative strengths of the tendency to succeed and to avoid failure. When the tendency to succeed is stronger, as it is for individuals who have a high need to achieve, there is selective action. However, here there is a catch. Having a strong need for achievement does not mean that such individuals take up difficult tasks. The tasks which such individuals take up are moderately difficult in which the probability of success is reasonable and the pride of accomplishment fairly high! On the other hand when the tendency to avoid failure is dominant, the individual either prefers very simple tasks in which probability of failure is low or very difficult tasks where the humiliation of failure is less. In both cases we see either selective action or avoidance to take up tasks of specific difficulty levels – this is nothing but a subtle motivated act of task avoidance or procrastination. Thus achievement oriented or selective avoidance oriented both covertly contributes to acts of selective action, avoidance or procrastination.

Manufacturing Motivation: De-Motivating Procrastination

Many of us can have weak persistence, less than average self-discipline, or not enough courage in facing a task. Sometimes we feel the pay-off will be worth the effort…and sometimes we aren't sure! But we can help ourselves *act,* which is what *motivation,* is all about! We need to strengthen motivation in a positive sense of the term and thereafter de-motivate procrastination.

Maintain A Logbook of Your Works: Keep a record of all that you have to do, highlight your estimate of success or failure on those tasks, perceived level of difficulty, against its actual difficulty during executing the works and rate of success or failure. Now once you have gathered such a data sit down and statistically analyse it – I am sure you have imagined more of the negatives but attained more of the positives related with that task. One's imagination can surely drive him crazy – but think positive and attain positive results. Procrastinate negatives. Activate the positives.

Rebuke Your Lame Excuses: Many people are in a habit of making lame excuses to justify incomplete works. The chain of such a habit is too weak to be felt until it gets too strong to be broken. So watch out before it is too late. Baseless excuses will not help you in any manner. List out your tasks and before each put down your excuse. Now become your own boss and one by one counter the excuses you have made. Don't you feel that the boss is always right? Give your lame excuse a crunch and make it run away! Cure the lame procrastination!

Confront Your Fear of Failure: One always fears the unknown so familiarize yourself with it. This familiarization with the unknown will definitely be the stepping stone in combating your fear of failure. Make a descending hierarchical list of your fears. This list will help expose your distorted thought pattern and enable you to format ways to cope with the same. Now begin by analysing your worst fear. Does this fear seem real or is it only a fragment of your imagination? If it actually appears real then try identifying ways and means to overcome it. Once you think with a composed mind you surely will get a grip over your fears one by one by working out your own strategies to cope with them. A deep lurking fear is nothing but an obstruction you must overcome. Once the obstruction is cleared you will start procrastinating your fear of failure and see your goal directed activities get a new boost.

Pat Your Own Back: Each day before going to sleep in the night reflect on whatever you have done and achieved – even the smallest of achievement. Feel proud of even your smallest achievements. This patting of your own back will give a boost to your self-confidence. This small gesture may seem like blowing your own trumpet in private but it will be music to the ears of others when it shows results in your task oriented behaviour. Pat away your procrastination!

List Out Your Daily Activities: Listing your daily activities will help you break free from a lethargy cycle and get you motivated again for basic activity. This routine will not only ready you for the task to be done but also create within you an enthusiasm to do it.. However, here too list your tasks on the basis of priority. Classify them into work or pleasure activity. Now make sure that your top list does not only contain work and more work – all work and no play can push you to procrastinate work. Remember to rate your works and see the pleasure you feel in their accomplishment – enjoy through work as well!

Disarm Your Critics: This requires responding tactfully to your pushy critics who are always there giving you a piece of their advice.

Although the critics may have good advice, when it is pushy, it is proper for you to push back and cut off your nose to spite your face. Instead, to use this technique, you disarm the critic by agreeing with him, but then you own the decision. If your critic cares about your well being, this will result in a winning situation for you. You will no longer procrastinate work out of fear of criticism.

Take One Step At A Time: A journey of a thousand miles begins with a single step. You gradually progress and reach your final destination. You cannot complete any journey in a single leap. When confronted with overwhelming tasks or an overwhelming backlog, you simply cannot finish it in one go. You need to scale down the task into appropriate components. Thereafter divide the task into manageable units assigning a time limit for its completion. You may assign any time which you feel is within the comfortable range but don't give too much of a time margin – it will begin running late and also your interest may fade away. Thus, step by step you will not only be moving towards attaining your goal but your procrastination will be taking a retreat.

Motivate Your Motivation: Example, I must do this. I should do this. I ought to do this. A good start is half the battle won. Begin any task with a positive mindset. Always be very clear as to what you have to do and why you have to do it. The drive to accomplish is always need based and the need should be felt very distinctively. Feeling this need will show you your goal clearly and at the same time guide your efforts in attaining that goal. Keeping this positive attitude and being clear about what and why you have to do so will help reinforce your motivation from not procrastinating.

Rate Your Pleasures: Make a list of your numerous activities which gives you pleasure. After having made the list, grade these activities on a ten point scale. Give a ten to the activity which brings you maximum pleasure in terms of satisfaction. After doing this predictive exercise, keep a log of any such activity you indulge in.

After engaging in that activity put down your ratings in terms of actual satisfaction obtained using the same ten point scale. When you assess your actual satisfaction, you get feedback on how well you are predicting what will make you happy or bring you pleasure. Getting correct feedback will motivate you to indulge in that recreational activity more often. This satisfaction will relax you and you will find that it will also positively benefit your task oriented behaviour.

Indulge In Self-Endorsement: Are you in a habit of undervaluing your efforts? Do you perceive your outputs worthless? Do you always keep thinking about what you failed to accomplish? If the answers to the above questions are affirmative then you need to seriously indulge in self-endorsement. Man often becomes what he believes himself to be. If you consistently say to yourself that you cannot do a certain thing, it is possible that you may really become incapable of doing it. On the contrary, if you inculcate a belief that you can do it, you will surely acquire the capacity to do it even if you did not have it at the beginning. Learn to blow your own trumpet but for yourself only. How to bring this music to your ears is very easy indeed. Never perceive your outputs to be worthless – they are the outcome of your praiseworthy efforts. Never get dejected with your failures. Always focus on your accomplishments and work towards overcoming your failures. By self-endorsing yourself you will feel rejuvenated and begin enjoying your work rather than procrastinating it.

Stay Focused On What You Are Doing: A positive way of achieving improvement in your work output is to focus on what you are doing and not on the result that is being produced at that time. Perhaps your concentration on the outcome distracts your input. All you need to do is focus on what you are doing and how you are doing it rather than on the output that is being produced. This shift of attention will help ease your work and also lead to a better output. Always focus on what you are doing and the output will take care of itself.

Don't Think. Prove Your Thoughts: Many a time you get obsessed with negative thought patterns which de-motivates you and so you procrastinate work. If you are obsessed with such negative thought patterns then don't only think, prove to yourself that you can do what you think you cannot. Don't test your inability altogether – distribute the task into its basic components and do it at a comfortable pace – don't keep time limits but then also don't prolong unnecessarily. You will find that in most instances things you thought could not be done by you are things which you could do quite well and comfortably – it's all in the mind.

Visualize Your Victory: The best and easiest way anyone can motivate himself (at least temporarily) is imagining being a successful victorious hero. Picture yourself being given accolades for the great tasks you have done. This temporary visual of your successful self will help enhance your self-esteem superficially but nonetheless will give you just enough motivation to go ahead in initiating the task which you have so far been procrastinating. A good start will also lead to successful accomplishment with the right combination of methods of de-motivating procrastination.

In concluding this chapter what I would like to finally say is that it is all in your mind. You need to get control over your thought pattern and your actions will take care of the rest. Positive thinking will help alter your perspective and you will begin to see the works you had been procrastinating in a new dimension – a dimension showing the possibility of its attainment. So get ready to self-motivate yourself as my words alone cannot do any magic. Forty people can take a horse to the well but they cannot make him drink – the horse needs to be thirsty. You need to force within you the desire to overcome procrastination till this desire generates the necessary motivating forces within you. So get set and go to de-motivate your procrastination.

❑❑❑

12

Personality And Procrastination

"Look to see what you are doing today.
Is this how you choose to define yourself?
Look to see what you are thinking today.
Is this what you wish to create?"

This chapter is going to sum up how procrastination relates with an individual's personality. You have already seen that procrastination is considered as the tendency to postpone in numerous situations that are necessary to reach goals and affects approximately 20–25% of the adult population in various countries. So many researches across the globe have opined that procrastination is complex and comprise distinct personality traits. They concluded that, self-reported procrastination positively correlated with extroversion, and had a curvilinear relationship with neuroticism – high and low scores positively associated with higher procrastination scores. Procrastination may also be linked to the Big-Five model of personality. Within that model, two main personality traits, neuroticism and conscientiousness, appear to be linked to procrastination. It has been found that neuroticism, and especially the underlying facets of impulsiveness and vulnerability, are a significant predictor of procrastination among university students. Research has also found that strong neuroticism is a predictor of procrastination, adding depression and self-consciousness facets to it. However, extensive research has come to the conclusion that low conscientiousness is the overall strongest predictor of procrastination. Taken together, these findings supported other studies reporting that low conscientiousness, specifically, low self-discipline, strongly predicted procrastination. Additional research into the relation between low conscientiousness and procrastination indicated that higher procrastination related to lower persistence in pursuing and organization.

Before I take you into an in-depth tour of your personality traits, let me help you measure them so that you become aware about their degree of presence or absence within you. This awareness will help you relate them better with the problem of procrastination – if at all you have one. The personality test below is based upon the Big Five model of personality and has only limited questions to roughly measure the presence/absence of these in your personality.

Measure Your Personality Traits

Below are given a few statements and you have to respond in agreement or disagreement with the statement. Kindly be very honest with your responses.

Openness to Experience (O)

1. I have a rich vocabulary. *Yes/No.*
2. I have a vivid imagination. Yes/No.
3. I have excellent ideas. *Yes/No.*
4. I am quick to understand things. *Yes/No.*
5. I use difficult words. *Yes/No.*
6. I spend time reflecting on things. *Yes/No.*
7. I am full of ideas. *Yes/No.*
8. I am interested in abstractions. *Yes/No.*
9. I am creatively imaginative. *Yes/No.*
10. I easily understand abstract ideas. *Yes/No.*

Total: ☐

Conscientiousness (C)

1. I am always prepared for anything. *Yes/No.*
2. I pay attention to details. *Yes/No.*
3. I get chores done right away. *Yes/No.*
4. I like order. *Yes/No.*
5. I follow a schedule. *Yes/No.*
6. I do my work very thoroughly. *Yes/No.*
7. I keep my things very organized. *Yes/No.*
8. I keep my surroundings neat and clean. *Yes/No.*
9. I keep back things where they are to be kept. *Yes/No.*
10. I willingly do my duties. *Yes/No.*

Total: ☐

Extroversion (E)

1. I am the life of the party. *Yes/No.*
2. I don't mind being the centre of attention. *Yes/No.*
3. I feel comfortable around people. *Yes/No.*
4. I start conversations readily. *Yes/No.*
5. I talk to a lot of different people at parties. *Yes/No.*
6. I am very talkative. *Yes/No.*
7. I like being in the limelight. *Yes/No.*
8. I have a lot to say. *Yes/No.*
9. I like being the focus of attention. *Yes/No.*
10. I readily make conversations with strangers. *Yes/No.*

Total: ☐

Agreeableness (A)

1. I am interested in people. *Yes/No.*

2. I sympathize with others' feelings. *Yes/No.*
3. I have a soft heart. *Yes/No.*
4. I take time out for others. *Yes/No.*
5. I feel others' emotions. *Yes/No.*
6. I make people feel at ease. *Yes/No.*
7. I am interested in others. *Yes/No.*
8. I respect people. *Yes/No.*
9. I am interested in knowing about other people's problems. *Yes/No.*
10. I feel concerned for others. *Yes/No.*

Total: ☐

Neuroticism (N)

1. I am easily disturbed. *Yes/No.*
2. I change my mood a lot. *Yes/No.*
3. I get irritated easily. *Yes/No.*
4. I get stressed out easily. *Yes/No.*
5. I get upset easily. *Yes/No.*
6. I have frequent mood swings. *Yes/No.*
7. I often feel blue. *Yes/No.*
8. I worry about things. *Yes/No.*
9. I am never contented with anything. *Yes/No.*
10. I am tensed most of the time. *Yes/No.*

Total: ☐

Scoring and Interpretation

After you have marked your responses give a point of 1 each to every ***Yes*** you have ticked and a point of 0 to every ***No*** you have ticked. Now total up the scores for each segment separately and note them in the space provided. *Do not come to any conclusion with the high and low value of your obtained scores unless you read in detail the explanation for each of the factors given further ahead.* If you have obtained a score between **7-10** you are *high* on that particular factor, between **4-6** you are *moderate* and between **0-3** you are *low*. The factors are decoded and explained below in detail. Suggestions about how to improve upon those personality traits which are not only causing you to procrastinate but are also being harmful, are explained. So read ahead, become familiar and then change those personality traits which are harming you seriously.

YOUR PERSONALITY AND PROCRASTINATION: AKE THE NECESSARY CORRECTIONS

- **Openness To Experience (O)**: Openness is a general appreciation for art, emotion, adventure, unusual creative ideas, imagination, curiosity, and variety of experience. People who are open to experience are intellectually curious, appreciative of art, and sensitive to beauty. They tend to be, compared to closed people, more creative and more aware of their feelings. They are more likely to hold unconventional beliefs.

  People with low scores on openness tend to show more conventional, traditional interests. They prefer the plain, straightforward, and obvious over the complex, ambiguous, and subtle. They may view arts and sciences with suspicion or even disregard these endeavours as uninteresting.

  For Openness to Experience, the fantasy facet has been found as positively related to procrastination: the more fantasy, the higher the procrastination.

  My suggestion for individuals who have scored low on openness to experience is that they should wake up and be in touch with reality. Living in a world of fantasy will stunt their outlook and slow them from concretely executing their ideas. They will keep everything in life procrastinated. So wake up, be realistic and change your dreams into reality.

- **Conscientiousness (C)**: Conscientiousness is a tendency to show self-discipline, act dutifully, and aim for achievement against measures or outside expectations, a virtue that shows preference for planned, rather than spontaneous behaviour. It influences the way in which we control, regulate, and direct our impulses.

  If you have scored high on this then you need not be concerned about it influencing procrastination, if at all you are a procrastinator.

  However, if you have scored low on this measure then beware because low conscientiousness is the strongest indicator of procrastination. The lower your conscientiousness score, the higher your procrastination. In fact, all of the facets of conscientiousness are correlated with lower procrastination, including: Competence (efficient), Order (organized), Dutifulness (not careless), Achievement striving (thorough), Self-discipline (not lazy), and Deliberation (not impulsive). (Lack of) Self-discipline is the strongest facet-level predictor of procrastination. Given the very strong relation between Conscientiousness and procrastination, conscientiousness can be termed as the "source trait" of the lower-order trait of procrastination.

  It is a tough situation for you because you will have to change many features which are easy to suggest but difficult to change. To begin with it is your competence. In essence, procrastination is a form of incompetence. To cure it, is to eliminate it. Since incompetence is the opposite or lack of competence, *the only way to eliminate it is to replace it with competence.*

If you are low in competence you need to enhance it by following some tips. To begin with, prepare a list of your outstanding competencies and then alongside that list those competencies you wish to improve upon. If you feel that you need to acquire new skills then go ahead and acquire them. You can join training programs or even take up full time study courses depending upon your requirements for enhancing your competence. For example, if your aim is to develop your communication skill, en-roll as a communications major. Study courses such as speech and mass media. Choose a minor or add another major if you wish to develop a wide array of competencies. If you are a professional you can also improve upon your competencies via work experience. Obtaining first-hand experience is one of the surest ways to strengthen your desired skill. Be very attentive on the job and ask questions when you are unsure of how to do something. Furthermore, you can develop competencies by practicing and rehearsing. When you wish to improve your leadership skills, begin to practice qualities such as assertiveness, creativity and confidence. Assume roles and positions that require you to display the above qualities.

You also need to begin being organized in your life and work. Organized schedules will enhance your output while saving even your time and energy. This saved time and energy can be channelized into completing all your pending tasks. Try to awaken your conscience, give due importance to your duties, be thorough with your work, be self-disciplined, and avoid impulsiveness. All these together and even singly can defeat procrastination. So pull up your socks, put on your boots and stomp out procrastination from within you.

- **Extroversion (E)**: High scores on this, indicate that you are an extrovert. Extroversion is characterized by positive emotions, surgency, and the tendency to seek out stimulation and the company of others. The trait is marked by pronounced engagement with the external world. Extroverts enjoy being with people, and are often perceived as full of energy. They tend to be enthusiastic, action-oriented individuals who are likely to say "Yes!" or "Let's go!" to opportunities for excitement. In groups, they like to talk, assert themselves, and draw attention to themselves. The good news is that the hyper energy of extroverts signifies less procrastination.

  Low scores on this indicate that you are an introvert who lacks the social exuberance and activity levels of extroverts. You tend to be quiet, low-key, deliberate, and less involved in the social world. Your lack of social involvement should not be interpreted as shyness or depression. Introverts simply need less stimulation than extroverts and more time alone. They may be very active and energetic, but simply not social. The lower level of energy in introverts can, to some extent, influence and favour a procrastinating tendency in such individuals, although not necessarily.

  Being an introvert is not very self-rewarding. One tends to cut away from social activities, remain aloof and solitary. Since one is not very active socially, there also is a lack of drive and energy. This low energy at times, also affects the outcome of tasks at hand. Introversion is a characteristic which is quite rigid and not easily open to modification. However, if you are an introvert and you find that you are also in the habit of procrastinating then you need to pay special attention towards doing your work on time. You need to create within you the desire which will drive you towards task accomplishment. Where there is a need there is a drive and where there is a drive there is energy for action which leads to accomplishment – social or unsocial, be friendly with your work.

- **Agreeableness (A)**: High scores show that you are agreeable. Agreeableness is a tendency to be compassionate and cooperative rather than suspicious and antagonistic towards others. The trait reflects an individual's indifference towards social harmony. Agreeable individuals' value interaction with others. They are generally considerate, friendly, generous, helpful, and willing to compromise their interests for others. Agreeable people also have an optimistic view of human nature. They believe people are basically honest, decent, and trustworthy.

  Low scores indicate disagreeableness. Disagreeable individuals place self-interest above getting along with others. They are generally unconcerned with others' well-being, and are less likely to reach out to other people. Sometimes their scepticism about other's motives compels them to be suspicious, unfriendly, and uncooperative.

  Agreeableness or disagreeableness in no way appears to be related with procrastination so worry not about this in relation with procrastination.

- **Neuroticism (N)**: High scores indicate a tendency towards Neuroticism. This is a tendency to experience negative emotions, such as anger, anxiety, or depression. It is sometimes called emotional instability. Those who score high in neuroticism are emotionally reactive and vulnerable to stress. They are more likely to interpret ordinary situations as threatening, and minor frustrations as hopelessly difficult. Their negative emotional reactions tend to persist for unusually long periods of time, which means they often remain in a bad mood. These problems of emotional regulation can diminish the ability of a neurotic person to think clearly, make decisions, and cope effectively with stress. Individuals high on neuroticism are more susceptible to its influence on procrastination, especially the strongest facet-level predictor being impulsiveness and perfectionism. The relationship of procrastination with perfectionism has already been discussed earlier.

Impulsiveness is a multi-factorial construct that involves a tendency to act on a whim, displaying behaviour characterized by little or no forethought, reflection, or consideration of consequences. Impulsive actions typically are "poorly conceived, prematurely expressed, unduly risky, or inappropriate to the situations that often result in undesirable consequences," which imperil long term goals and strategies for success. If you are prone to impulsiveness then it may also be affecting your task outputs. You may be procrastinating doing things. This procrastination is the result of a frustration being experienced by you which leads to impulsive behaviour and results in tasks remaining unfinished. – starting with a bang and not ending at all! Take your time to complete the task rather than feel rushed to end it. This rushing attitude is a result of frustration being suffered by you which, in turn leads to your impulsive behaviour. When confronted with any such situation, take a deep breath, relax and think before you begin doing that task. This small exercise will relax your anxiety level and help you successfully accomplish the task.

In concluding this chapter, all I would like to stress upon is that, because of your procrastinating nature you must try improvising upon the weaknesses in your personality. You should try to develop into a mentally healthy individual creating around you an atmosphere which emits positive sparks. ***Procrastination,*** *if it is there in you, should be* ***procrastinated*** *forever and you should try emerging as a total winner in all that you do. You are only one, you cannot do everything but still you can do something and because you cannot do everything you will not refuse to do the something that you can do. My words alone cannot make you a perfect and healthy individual but your determination and efforts sure can help you achieve great heights in life. So make it your mission to strive for attaining what you have always desired in your life for yourself and your loved ones. Once you have made up your mind and have a strong determination, even the strongest of procrastinating factors cannot make you deter from your path – it is all in the mind and the mind is all yours and under your control – so control your life and make it worthy.*